David T.

P9-DBK-230

The Lorette Wilmot Library
and Media Center
Nazareth College of Rochester

Amyntas

&

The Lamentations of Amyntas

VOLUME II OF THE PUBLICATIONS

OF THE RENAISSANCE ENGLISH TEXT SOCIETY

Thomas Watson's Latin

Amyntas

(1585)

EDITED BY WALTER F. STATON, JR.

&

Abraham Fraunce's Translation

The Lamentations of Amyntas

(1587)

EDITED BY FRANKLIN M. DICKEY

Published by

The University of Chicago Press

for

The Newberry Library

Library of Congress Catalog Card Number: 66-14114

THE UNIVERSITY OF CHICAGO PRESS, CHICAGO & LONDON
The University of Chicago Press, Ltd., London W.C.1.

© 1967 by The University of Chicago
All rights reserved. Published 1967
Second Impression 1968
Printed in the United States of America

IN MEMORIAM

William Alexander Jackson, 1905–1964
Vice President, Renaissance English Text Society

Robert Cecil Bald, 1901–1965
Chairman of the Editorial Committee, Renaissance English Text Society

Contents

Introduction / ix

Facsimile of Watson's Title Page / 1

Watson's Dedication to Henry Noel / 2

Facsimile of Watson's *Ad Lectorem* / 6

Facsimile of Fraunce's Title Page / 7

Fraunce's Dedication to the Countess of Pembroke / 8

Amyntas / 10

The Lamentations of Amyntas / 11

Epigram / 90

Appendix / 93

Introduction

I

Thomas Watson, whose *Amyntas* here reprinted survives
only in a unique copy in the British Museum, was one of the
most admired of the later Elizabethan poets. Between 1589
and 1607 there were references to him, mostly laudatory, in
at least fifteen printed volumes,[1] and in the same period in-
dividual poems or quotations from poems by Watson appeared in nine volumes.[2] While the quotations are mainly,
but not entirely, from his English works, the bulk of the references link him with his Latin *Amyntas*, which is certainly
the work, of the ten of his that are extant and identified, for
which he was best known.

Several errors concerning the present work and its author
have been more or less current. Thomas Watson (*ca.* 1555–
1592), the poet and author of *Amyntas*, has often been con-
fused with Thomas Watson (*ca.* 1515–1584), Bishop of Lincoln and author of the Latin tragedy *Absalom*. Even more
often Watson's *Amyntas* has been called a translation of
Tasso's play *Aminta*, though it is an entirely different and
independent work. Edward Arber in his 1870 edition of Watson's English poems surmised incorrectly that the poem beginning "Aurora now began to rise" in *The Phoenix Nest* and

[1] Nashe in Greene's *Menaphon* (1589); Lodge, *Scillaes Metamorphosis*
(1589); Spenser, *Faerie Queene* (1590), *Complaints* (1591); G. Harvey,
Foure Letters (1592); Peele, *The Honour of the Garter* (1593); Richard Barn-
field, *The Affectionate Shepheard* (1594); John Dickenson, *The Shepherds
Complaint* (1596); William Covell, *Polimanteia* (1595); Thomas Edwards,
Cephalus and Procris (1595); Nashe, *Have With You to Saffron-Walden*
(1596); *Ulisses on Ajax* (1596); Francis Meres, *Palladis Tamia* (1598); *The
Returne from Pernassus* (1606); Dekker, *A Knights Conjuring* (1607).

[2] William Vallans, *A Tale of Two Swannes* (1590); *The Honorable En-
tertainment ... at Elvetham* (1591); *The Phoenix Nest* (1593); Charles Fitz-
Geffrey, *Sir Francis Drake* (1596); *Englands Helicon* (1600); Francis Da-
vison, *A Poetical Rhapsody* (1602); Francis Pilkington, *The First Booke of
Songs or Ayres* (1605); Robert Allott, *Englands Parnassus* (1606); William
Byrd, *Psalmes, Songs, and Sonnets* (1611).

[*ix*]

Introduction

Englands Helicon was Watson's own translation of "Querela octaua" of *Amyntas*. In Warren B. Austin, "Thomas Watson's Adaptation of an Epigram by Martial," *RN*, XIII (1960), 134–40, the "Olus" in the epigram appended to *Amyntas* is identified as Gabriel Harvey, primarily on the basis of a mistranslation of line 12, "Forsan at exemplis linea nulla caret," as "but at least no line is missing from the printed texts," which should be translated, "still there is no line without a precedent." Finally, the attribution to Watson of the 1593 volume of poems entitled *The Tears of Fancie* has now been shown to rest mainly on a Collier forgery.[3]

Part of the high reputation Watson enjoyed among his contemporaries undoubtedly stems from his mere display of learning. Prior to 1581 he had spent some seven years of study in France and Italy, and he shows throughout his writing a broad and up-to-date acquaintance with the literary developments in those countries as well as with classical Latin and Greek literature. In the epigram appended to *Amyntas* Watson says that his verse has been attacked as metrically defective but that he has precedents for every line. As far as *Amyntas* is concerned this is probably true. He has occasional badly placed caesuras, but apart from X, 17, which is marked, there seem to be no defective verses or liberties taken without classical warrant. Watson's Latin is also more correct by Ciceronian standards than that of most of his contemporaries. The only postclassical words I have noted are: *labile* (I, 10), *blandisonis* (I, 33), *taxicolae* (I, 77), *formosula* (IV, 45), *recipiscere* (VIII, 96), *serate* (XI, 25). Watson's main departures from classical grammatical practice are likewise few. Apart from certain liberties with tenses, they amount to *stertam* (I, 87) and *haeret* (IV, 10) used as tran-

---

[3] The best account of the life and works of Thomas Watson, the poet, is in Mark Eccles, *Christopher Marlowe in London* (Cambridge, Mass., 1934); the best account of the bishop is in *A Humanist's "Trew Imitation": Thomas Watson's Absalom*, ed. John Hazel Smith (Urbana, 1964). Many people, e.g., Leicester Bradner, *Musae Anglicanae* (New York, 1940), have called attention to the independence of Watson's *Amyntas* from Tasso's *Aminta*. Arber's error was corrected by W. W. Greg, "English Versions of Watson's Latin Poems," *MLQ*, VI (1903), 125–29. Franklin Dickey, "Forgeries in the Stationers' Register," *SQ*, XI (1960), 39–47, revealed the Collier forgery.

sitive verbs; *fuerint . . . peracta* (III, 91) and *erepta fuisset*
(IV, 72), where classical practice calls for the future and
imperfect forms of the auxiliary; and the indicative *ducit*
in an indirect question (IV, 19). We may suppose, however,
that in these pastoral hexameters Watson was on his good
linguistic behavior, for in his prose *Compendium Memoriae
Localis*,[4] written almost certainly in the same year as *Amyntas*, he is much less Ciceronian.

Part of Watson's reputation probably stems from his asso-
ciation with the artistic avant-garde of his day. Eccles has
demonstrated in *Christopher Marlowe in London* (1934) his
close friendship with Marlowe. The commendatory poems to
his *Hecatompathia* (1582) suggest Watson's connection with
Peele, Royden, and Atchelow. Both Nashe and Barnfield
refer to him as a friend and mentor. He seems also to have
been acquainted in musical circles. He wrote a laudatory
poem about John Case's *The Praise of Musicke* (1586). At
his request William Byrd wrote two madrigals for *The First
Sett of Italian Madrigalls Englished* (1590). Moreover the
dedicatee of *Amyntas* as well as of *Compendium Memoriae
Localis*, Henry Noel (d. 1597), who is credited with a poem
in *Englands Helicon* and a distich against Ralegh, seems
also to have been a patron of music. At least, after his death
both Thomas Morley and Thomas Weelkes wrote madrigals
in Noel's memory.[5]

But the greatest reason for Watson's reputation is that he
introduced in the 1580's poetic methods and motifs which
were to become highly fashionable in the 1590's.[6] These
methods and motifs are exactly those of the Italian poets
of the late fifteenth and early sixteenth centuries, men like

[4] The *Short Title Catalogue* lists this work as by another Thomas Watson
than Thomas Watson the poet, but since in its dedication (which inci-
dentally is to the same Henry Noel as that of the present work) the author
refers to "noster Amintas," there can be no doubt that both works are
by the same author.

[5] I am indebted for my information about Noel as well as for a number
of other points to Professor William Ringler.

[6] Hallett Smith, *Elizabethan Poetry* (Cambridge, Mass., 1952), pp. 133–
38, has an account of the importance of Watson's 1582 *Hecatompathia*
in this respect.

Serafino, Sannazaro, Molza, and the Strozzi. (I should note, however, that though I have searched fairly diligently, I have found only one unacknowledged borrowing from these writers in any of Watson's works, and this is in the 1592 *Amintae Gaudia* from Tito Strozzi and is really more an expansion of a theme than a direct borrowing.)[7] The basis of Watson's technique is strict limitation of form and subject. In *Amyntas* the eleven "querelae" were probably intended to contain 100 lines each—"prima" has 99 and "quarta" 98, but this may be owing to error by either Watson or the printer. Each of the first ten begins and ends with a verbal variation on the same idea, and each has the same subject, lament for the dead shepherdess. Thus limited, the poet shows his inventiveness by his variety of treatment. He has at his disposal all the rhetorical devices, ranging from the various figures of word repetition to elaborate similes and apostrophes and such specialized devices as the Virgilian list of impossibilities at VIII, 79–80. For matter he can draw upon the rich field of classical myth and on the less rich area of the traditional shepherd life with its conventional tasks, sports, and environment. It is the number of different ways in which he can introduce these devices and this matter that measures his success as a poet. As an example of the method we might consider "Querela quarta." The bulk of this lament consists of a series of apostrophes to the Thames nymphs, Sylvanus, Cupid, and Tellus, the personification of earth. In the last of these, lines 51–76, the point is that the earth should be sad because Phyllis is no longer on it. Fraunce mistranslates lines 54–55, "portasti toties et amabile pondus corporis" ("you have often borne the lovely weight of her body"), as "Whose sweet corps thou bar'st," because he is thinking of another way in which an apostrophe to the earth can be made relevant to Phyllis' death. But Watson had already used this idea, that the earth should be happy to contain Phyllis' body, at III, 37 ff. In "Querela quarta" Watson is thinking of the earth's sorrow and introduces two myths, the gigantomachia and the rape of Proserpina, to

[7] *Strozii Poetae Pater et Filius* (Venice, 1513), ff. 20ᵛ–21 and Watson, *Amintae Gaudia* (London, 1592), I2ᵛ–4.

reinforce his idea. Such methods and motifs were the vogue in the 1590's.

Watson's translator, Abraham Fraunce, sympathized with this vogue, and his sins of translation result generally from an excess of zeal rather than a failure to understand his author's intention. In assessing Fraunce's translation, one hardly needs to notice the dozen or so literal errors of the type cited above. Likewise simple condensations, expansions, and transpositions involving from two to five lines (and this is all we have) are to be expected from translators in all ages. More interesting are Fraunce's occasional additions and transmutations. At II, 16–17, for example, Watson has "Cur non balatis, cur non saltatis vt olim?|Quid pratis agni, Baccho quid parcitis hœdi?" ("Why don't you bleat, why don't you jump as formerly? Why do you lambs spare the meadows, you goats the vine?") Fraunce translates lines 15–17, "Your wont was, some part to be bleating, some to be skipping,|Some with bended browes and horned pates to be butting,|Sheepe to be gnapping grasse, and goats to the vines to be climing." What Fraunce has in mind here is a common pastoral motif which derives ultimately, I believe, from Virgil's *Culex*, lines 48–57, a description of groups of sheep variously occupied. Watson was not thinking of this motif, but it is thoroughly consonant with his poetic method. A greater distortion is Fraunce's overuse of the figures of word repetition. In "Querela octaua" Fraunce links forty-three lines by anaphora compared to Watson's eleven, and Fraunce's use of epistrophe quite o'erflows the measure.

DESCRIPTION

[85] [Within a border of type ornaments] AMYNTAS| *Thomæ VVatsoni*|Londinensis|*I. V. studiosi.*|[type ornament]|*Nemini datur amare simùl*|*et sapere.*|*EXCVDEBAT*| |Henricus Marsh, ex|*assignatione Thomæ*|*Marsh*|1585.| [type ornament]

π⁴, A-C⁸. Preliminary gathering of four leaves unsigned, first three leaves of each of the three octavo gatherings signed. Running titles: π2ᵛ–4 Epistola|dedicatoria. A1ᵛ–C6ᵛ Querela

prima. [secunda, etc.], C7ᵛ Epigramma. Catchwords regular
except for: π3ᵛ humani-|humanitatis, π4 [none], π4ᵛ [none],
A3ᵛ Qualis|"Qualis, A4 Nì|Nî, B2 Impedit| "Impedit, B5
"Laurea|Laurea, B5ᵛ Quid|"Quid, B6 Oreque|"Oreque, B8ᵛ
Iamque|Iamque, C6ᵛ [none]. A circular woodcut of Henricus
Rex (see facsimile p. 6), appears on π4ᵛ and C7ᵛ. STC 23691.
Not entered in the Stationers' Register. The unique copy is
British Museum C.83.a.19.(4.).

The book was printed by Henry Marsh, the assignee of
his father, Thomas Marsh. The latter had been one of the
most prominent English printers in the 1560's and 1570's
and had become an upper warden in the Stationers' Company in 1580, but after 1582 he registered no books and published very few, although he was apparently still active in
1587. Henry Marsh published only one other book, *The
Mirror for Magistrates* in 1587, "At London in Fleete streete,
by Henry Marsh, being the assigne of Thomas Marsh." A
comparison of the ornamental types in *Amyntas* with those
in other Marsh books makes it clear that it also came from
the paternal shop. On 23 June 1591 another son, Edward
Marsh, transferred *Amyntas* and ninety-one other books
belonging to Thomas Marsh, now deceased, to Thomas
Orwyn. There is no indication, however, that Watson's
Latin poem received a second printing.

The following text of *Amyntas* is set up from a microfilm
of the unique copy in the British Museum, to the authorities
of which thanks are extended for permission to reprint. The
italic of the original has been changed to roman. Abbreviations (&, q;, and macron over vowel) have been expanded
silently. Accent marks are used in the original in the following way: circumflex indicates a long vowel and is used generally for homographs and contractions, "mâlas," "usurpâ-
rit"; grave indicates an adverb, "publicè," "quìn"; acute
indicates a shift in syllable stress, "montésque"; in expanding
q; the accent has been moved to the preceding vowel. The
copy text has been reproduced *literatim* except for the correction of a few obvious errors that are noted in the apparatus at
the foot of the page. Woodcut initial capitals have not been
reproduced.   WALTER F. STATON, JR.

II

Abraham Fraunce's English hexameters appeared in four separate editions between 1587 and 1596 and in a fifth as "The Second Part" of *The Countesse of Pembrokes Yuychurch* (1591). If Fraunce's *Lamentations* cannot rival the eight Elizabethan editions of Daniel's *Delia* or the ten of Shakespeare's *Venus and Adonis*, they did achieve a success with Elizabethan bookbuyers equal to or greater than that of poets we prize more highly today. The *Short Title Catalogue* lists the same number of editions for *The Shepheardes Calender*. Breton's *Bowre* (1591, 1597) went out of print with two editions, Spenser's *Amoretti and Epithalamion* (1595) with one. But after 1596 Fraunce is forgotten save in Ben Jonson's words to Drummond, "That Abram Francis jn his English Hexameters was a Foole".[1]

Jonson, of course, was right: there could be no future for quantitative verse and anyone writing it condemned himself to oblivion. However, Fraunce's verses are of some historical interest and serve handsomely to show the possibilities as well as the limitations of "quantities" in English. Certainly Fraunce's are among the most plausible attempts to write at length in imitation of Latin metrics.

Although there is not room in this introduction for extended demonstration, Fraunce's verses can be scanned if one wishes to follow his lead. He left no instructions, but his practice follows what little we know of "Master Drant's rules," at least as they appear in Sidney's note in the margin of the *Arcadia*, St. John's College, Cambridge, Manuscript 308.[2] Since Sidney's rules, though elliptical, serve as the best external guide to reading Fraunce, I summarize and interpret from Ringler's transcript of them. If it is impossible to follow these directions altogether literally because their description of English sounds is far from scientific, their general intent

[1] *Conversations with Drummond*, in *Ben Jonson*, ed. C. H. Herford and Percy Simpson (Oxford, 1925), I, 133. The best general introduction to Fraunce's life and works is the "Introduction" to G. C. Moore Smith's edition of Fraunce's *Victoria* in Bang's *Materialien* XIV (Louvain, 1906).

[2] See the article by William Ringler, "Master Drant's Rules," *PQ*, XXIX (1950), 70–74, in which these rules are printed for the first time.

may be pieced together. The problem is complicated by the arbitrary nature of quantitative verse even in Latin but more especially in English. It is further complicated because Sidney (or Drant) may be confusing orthography and pronunciation. But if one makes an allowance for possible sixteenth-century pronunciation, the rules generally do make sense. In any event Fraunce can be scanned by them.

First, a vowel followed by two consonants is always long unless the consonants are "a mute and a liquid." Some consonants are considered to have a "dowble sownde"— *-ck*, *-ll*—and with their preceding vowels make a "long." Diphthongs in the same position are long, and the writer considers "show" and "blow" as well as "dye" and "hye" as diphthongs. Vowels (or diphthongs) before vowels (or diphthongs) are short, as are "single vowells," that is, vowels naturally short, not lengthened by position. Elision may occur when vowels meet, as "th'art" for "thow art." Words derived from Latin scan by their English quantity. "Particles"—*but, or, nor, on, to,* etc.—may be either long or short. The exclamation "Oh" is long.

Fraunce seems to expect his readers to disregard accent altogether and rely solely on quantity for the metrical pattern. Ictus and accent are thus often at odds as they are in Latin "artificial" verse. In order to make the reader aware of the quantity desired Fraunce often relies on spelling, though he seems to have been too sophisticated to suppose that spelling alone can make a line scan. It seems clear, however, that Fraunce's orthographical niceties are designed like Sidney's to help the reader give the syllables their proper arbitrary duration. Thus in the "faults escaped" he or the printer following his directions makes such changes as "outragious" to "outragius," "wofull" to "woful," "captein" to "capten," and "shall" to "shal." Other examples of spelling designed to aid scansion abound, such as "desperat outcries" (V, 12) or "meddows" (V, 18). Yet in editions after the first where compositors do not always respect the spellings of the original, the verse may still be scanned with little difficulty.

Rather than attempt a further synopsis of rules it seems

easier to show by means of examples how the verses may be read. As indicated, they should be read with normal accent but to regularly measured quantity, the long syllables receiving roughly twice the time of the short. Typical of the heavily monosyllabic lines of English hexameters—noted as a fault of the language in Sidney's "rules"—is the opening line:

In flowre | of young | yeares fayre | Phillis | lately de | parting.

The second and third show Fraunce's use of repetition for aural effects which imitate but go far beyond Watson's Latin:

With teares | continu | al was | daily be | wayld of A | myntas

halfe mad A | myntas, | careful A | mintas, | mournful A | mintas.[3]

Lines 14 and 15 show the richness of Fraunce's aural texture. The key words are given variety and emphasis by being put in different rhythmic contexts:

This grie | uous mour | ning, by the | shore, by the | sands, by the

| desert,

Desert, | sands, and | shore which | witnes | were to my | mourning.[4]

Line 29 illustrates his interest in the echo effect of *traductio* and *conduplicatio* emphasized by the quantities:

Either in | others | armes, stil | looking | either on | other.[5]

Despite the odds against success in this kind, Fraunce has managed to put together lines with enough objective basis to give a genuine illusion of Latin meter in English. The rhythms seem unnatural because we have no English tradi-

[3] Assiduo gemitu tristis lugebat Amyntas,
Mentis inops, plenus curæ, lachrymosus Amyntas.

[4] Ille meos questus per inania littora secum
Deferet. . . .

[5] Alter in alterius defixus lumina vultu.

tion to support them.[6] Sixteenth-century readers no doubt had their difficulties with English quantitative verse but had more to go on than we do. Elizabethan schoolboys learned quantities by rote from masters pronouncing Latin very much in the English fashion.[7] Such readers should have been able to hear Fraunce's rhythms with less effort than we do. The five editions suggest that they did.

Because of their extreme artificiality and because of the excessive number of spondees the verse becomes monotonous when read at length. Fraunce does his best to overcome this limitation by employing sound devices approved by precepts of rhetoric. The effect is aural and intellectual rather than emotional. Fraunce attempts to make his English as capable of ingenuity as Watson's sometimes more condensed Latin and even to outgo it wherever possible. It is a small triumph if at times irritatingly mannered, but it was recognized in its own day. Watson's original never went beyond the first edition.

DESCRIPTION

AND LIST OF EDITIONS

[A] *THE*|Lamentations of Amyn-|tas for the death of Phillis, para-|phrastically translated out of Latine in-|to English Hexameters by|*Abraham Fraunce.*|[J. Wolfe's device, McKerrow 242]|LONDON|Printed by Iohn Wolfe, for Thomas Newman,|and Thomas Gubbin. *Anno Dom.* 1587. ¶², A–D⁴, E². E² probably blank missing. A 2–4, B–D 1–3, E1 signed. Running titles: ¶2ᵛ The Epistle Dedicatorie, A1ᵛ–E1 *The first* [*second*, etc.] *Lamentation*. The following errors and variants in catchwords appear: A1 O|Sometimes, A3 which|

---

[6] Jonson complains that we do not in English observe quantity by position because of our own careless disregard of "artificial" verse. He promises to provide some "spurre and incitement" to composing such verses, but he never does. See *The English Grammar* (1640) in Herford and Simpson, *op. cit.*, VIII, 500–501.

[7] J. E. Sandys, *A History of Classical Scholarship* (Cambridge, 1908), II, 233–34, notes that Coryat pronounced *vita* with the English diphthong and that Scaliger, having listened politely for fifteen minutes to an Englishman's Latin, apologized without irony for not understanding any English.

Which, A4ᵛ Nymphes|Nimphs, B2 sweet|Sweete, B2ᵛ *The*|
The, C2 *Phillis*|Phillis, D1 And|*A*nd, D3 Perpe-|Perpetuall,
D4ᵛ VVels|Wells. STC 23692. Not entered in the Stationers'
Register. Huntington Library 56684; Bodleian 4°Z.3 Art. Seld.

[B] *THE*|Lamentations of A-|mintas for the death of|
Phillis:|Paraphrastically translated out of Latine in-|to Eng-
lish Hexameters, by|*Abraham Fraunce.*|(∵)|*Newelie Cor-
rected.*|[J. Charlewood's device, McKerrow 112β]|*AT LON-
DON*|Printed by Iohn Charle-wood, for Thomas|Newman
and Thomas Gubbin.|*Anno. Dom. 1588.*

§², A–D⁴, E². E2 probably blank missing. STC 23693. Not
entered in the Stationers' Register. Huntington Library
69591; Corpus Christi College, Oxford.

[C] THE|Lamentations of A-|*mintas for the death of*|
Phillis.|*Paraphrasticallie translated out of Latine in-*|to Eng-
lish Hexameters, by|*Abraham Fraunce.*|Newly Corrected.|
[R. Robinson's device, McKerrow 202γ]|AT LONDON
|Printed by *Robert Robinson*, for Thomas|Newman *and*
Thomas Gubbin.|ANNO. DOM. 1589.

A–E⁴. E4 probably blank missing. STC 23694. Not entered in the Stationers' Register. Bodleian Library Bliss A 84;
Huntington Library 59748; Dulwich College Library o. a. 5.

[D] THE|*Countesse of Pembrokes*|Yuychurch.|*Conteining
the affectionate*|life, and vnfortunate death of|Phillis *and*
Amyntas: *That in*|*a Pastorall; This in a Fune-*|rall: both in
English|*Hexameters.*|By ABRAHAM FRAVNCE.|[ornament]|
LONDON,|Printed by *Thomas Orwyn* for|*William Ponson-
by*, dwelling in|Paules Churchyard, at the|signe of the
Bishops|head.|1591. [Title page border used by T. Orwyn,
McKerrow and Ferguson 117.]

A–M⁴. The revised *Lamentations* occupy signatures G1–
L2. STC 11340. Entered in the Stationers' Register, 9 Feb-
ruary 1591. Copies are located in the following libraries:
Bodleian, British Museum, Chapin, Dyce, Folger, Harvard,
Huntington, John Rylands, Johns Hopkins, Lincoln Cathe-
dral, Newberry, Pforzheimer, University of Illinois, Wellesley
College, and Winchester College. In addition the copy from
the Silver collection was sold for the Newberry Library at
the Sotheby sale of 8 November 1965, item 128.

Introduction

[E] THE | Lamentations of A- | *mintas for the death of* | Phillis. *Paraphrastically translated out of Latine in-* | to English Hexameters, by | *Abraham Fraunce.* | Newly Corrected. | [T. Gubbin's device, McKerrow 284] | AT LONDON | Printed by *Robert Robinson*, for Thomas Gubbin. | Anno Domini. | 1596.

A–E⁴. E4 probably blank missing. STC 23695. Entered in the Stationers' Register to John Newbery, 12 June 1600. British Museum C 40. e. 65; Archbishop Marsh's Library, Dublin, Z 4. 1. 11/3; Folger Library 23695; University of Illinois.

There are five editions, printed 1587, 1588, 1589, 1591, and 1596. The edition of 1587 is the basis for 1588. The 1588 edition served as copy for 1589 and, except for the authorial changes noted below, for 1591. The 1589 edition served as copy for 1596. Each edition after 1587 adds errors and departs further than its predecessor from the orthography of the first edition.

In 1591 Fraunce published the *Lamentations* as "The Second Part" of *The Countesse of Pembrokes Iuychurch.* "The First Part" consists of an adaptation in English hexameters of Tasso's *Aminta.* In order to make Watson's non-dramatic laments an appropriate sequel to Tasso's pastoral play, Fraunce added transitional lines and an original eclogue titled "The Eleuenth Day." "The Epistle" for the first—and last—time acknowledges that the *Lamentations* are translated from Watson's Latin.[8]

Because Fraunce has made substantive changes—altering phrases, supplying new lines and canceling old, changing words and spellings—the text of 1591 presents interesting editorial problems. However, for the most part the text follows that of 1588 and reproduces its errors. It appears that the text of 1591 was set from a copy of 1588 in which

[8] The Epistle, altered passages, and new eclogue are found in the appendix to our edition, pp. 91–95. In 1590 Watson issued his Latin *Meliboeus* simultaneously with his own English translation of it, *An Eglogue Vpon the death of the Right Honorable Sir Francis Walsingham.* Annoyed that Fraunce had received the credit for the *Lamentations* and perhaps wishing for some of Fraunce's success, Watson writes in the English Epistle, "And I interpret my self, lest Melibæus [*sic*] in speaking English by another mans labour, should leese my name in his chaunge, as my *Amyntas* did."

the author had marked changes and from a manuscript of
the new "Eleuenth Day."⁹ Both the 1587 and 1591 texts are
substantive because 1591 contains authorial corrections, but
since 1591 represents the author's afterthoughts and since
1587 is generally more accurate, being free of the errors introduced in 1588, 1587 is the copy for this reprint. No edition has appeared since 1596.

The only consistent difference between 1587 and subsequent editions is the practice of italicizing proper names.
None is so treated in the first edition but they are regularly
italicized from 1588 on. Between the two extant copies of
1587 the only variants are that the Bodleian copy ends II,
22 with a period instead of a comma and in VIII, 101 ends
the line with a colon instead of a period. Two 1588 copies
exist. Between the three copies of 1589 no variants were
noted. Between the five copies of 1591 collated there were no
variants. There were no variants between the four known
copies of 1596.

The following text of the 1587 edition is set up from the
copy in the Huntington Library, to the authorities of which
thanks are extended for permission to reprint; but the facsimile of the title page is from the uncropped Bodleian Library
copy. Italics in the copy text have been preserved but the
italics of subsequent editions except for passages from 1591
recorded in the appendix have not been noted. Abbreviations
(ampersand and macron) have been silently expanded; otherwise the copy text has been reproduced *literatim* except for
"VV" for "W", changes of font for initial capitals, and the
correction of manifest errors noted at the foot of the page.

SIGLA

A 1587, Huntington Library 56684.
A′ 1587, Bodleian Library 4° Z.3 Art. Seld.
B 1588, Huntington Library 69591; Corpus Christi College, Ox.

⁹ At II, 31–33, 1591 seems to agree with 1589 (see apparatus). I
have not found any other very clearly substantive variants to indicate
that 1589 was used as a basis for the text and am at a loss to explain this
agreement. If more copies of 1588 were extant light might be shed on the
problem.

Introduction

C 1589, Bodleian Library Bliss A 84; Huntington Library 59748; Dulwich College o. a. 5.

D 1591, British Museum C 34. c. (1). Passages from this edition were collated with British Museum 80. a. 28(1); with Bodleian Ward 482 and 80 T 27 Art. Seld. and Malone 202(2). The other extant copies are listed in the Description and List of Editions above.

E 1596, British Museum C 40. e. 65; Archbishop Marsh's Library, Dublin Z 4. 1. 11/3; Folger Library 23695; University of Illinois.

In the apparatus A stands for both copies except at II, 22 and VIII, 101 where the only A' variants are listed. C stands for all copies of 1589 since no variants appear between the Huntington and Dulwich copies. E stands for all copies of 1596; there were no variants between copies.

FRANKLIN M. DICKEY

AMYNTAS

Thomæ VVatsoni

Londinenſis
I.V. ſtudioſi.

Nemini datur amare ſimùl et ſapere.

EXCVDEBAT
Henricus Marſh, ex
aſſignatione Thomæ
Marſj
1585.

Facsimile of the title page of Watson's *Amyntas*, 1585. Courtesy of the British Museum. Original, 4.7″ × 3.1″.

Henrico Noello,

VIRO NOBILITATIS

ac virtutum communione perinsigni

Thomas Watsonus

S. P. D.

Culpare soleo Gorgiam, etsi virum philosophum, qui scriptis et orationibus publicè probare voluit, nihil in rerum natura esse, quod sit: Et Zenonem illum, qui eadem et posse, et non posse fieri affirmauit: quìn etiàm et Melissum, qui cùm res infinitæ sint, rationes tamen inuenire conatus est, quibus demonstraret, vnum quiddam esse totam rerum vniuersita-
[π2ᵛ] tem. Longè etenìm tenuiùs horum vnusquísque disputabat,| quàm argumenti magnitudo postulabat, At quantò rectiùs illi, atque tutiùs, qui salem, apiculas, febrem, caluitiem, egestatem, et ignorantiam summis laudibus extulerunt? Nempè satis quidem intellexisse mihi videntur, difficile ac arduum sibi fore, de rebus luculentis, et omnium confessione præclaris, aliquid afferre in medium, quod nemo antè vsurpâ-rit: de rebus autem contemptis et humilibus verba facere tantò facilius, quantò grauitas leuitate, res seria ludis et iocis est laboriosior. Istorum ego sequutus opinionem, prudenter fortassè mihi fecisse videor, si consilio; fœliciter, si casu; quòd omissis paulùm grauioribus studijs, in syluestribus Amyntæ querelis tantillum operæ atque olei insumpserim. Ipse Romanorum olim sapientissimus à ratione diuersum non putabat

Cum pueris equitare in arundine longa.

[π3] Quìd etiam Homerum commemorem, qui pro|murium et ranarum pugna haud minori laude affectus est, quàm pro aureo illo Iliadis, aut Odyssææ monumento? Quìd Virgilium, qui Ænæidos et Culicis sui eandem ferè laudem reportauit? Quid deníque Petrarcham, (vt quamplurimos præteriam) qui cùm Lauræ mores et mortem iuueniliùs exposuisset, tamen

TRANSLATION OF THE DEDICATION

To Henry Noel,

a very noble and talented gentleman,

Thomas Watson sends best regards.

I always condemn Gorgias, although he was a philosopher, because he tried in his public writings and speeches to maintain that nothing in nature exists: and that Zeno who asserted that the same thing both can and cannot be done: and even more Melissus, who tried to prove that although matter is infinite, there is still a single, solid universe. Each one of them argued far more finely than the importance of his argument required. How much truer and safer are they who extolled so highly salt, bees, fever, baldness, poverty, and ignorance! For it seems to me that they knew it would be very difficult for them to publish anything that had not been done before on a striking and universally respected subject: for it is easier to write about base and contemptible subjects, just as gravity is harder than levity, a serious subject harder than jests and jokes. Following the second of these courses, I have probably been wise if by advice or lucky if by chance I neglected for a while my graver studies and spent a little work and midnight oil on these pastoral complaints of Amyntas. The wisest of Romans himself once did not think it unreasonable

To ride on a hobby horse with boys.

Shall I recall Homer, who was praised no less for the battle of the mice and frogs than for that golden monument of the *Iliad* or the *Odyssey*? Or Virgil, who earned almost the same praise for his *Aeneid* and his *Culex*? Or finally Petrarch (to pass over many others), who, after he had described in youthful fashion the character and the death of Laura, then wrote his famous *Trionfi*? I hope no one thinks, because I have

[*3*]

celeberrimos posteà Triumphos decantauit? Neminem verò
ex istis, quæ iam dixi, putare velim, me adeo φίλαυτον esse, et
insolentis animi, vt ausim existimare, vel cum Homeri Batrachomyomachia meas Querelas, vel cum Maronis Culice meum
Pastorem, vel cum Petrarchæ Laura Phyllida meam vlla ex
parte conferendam esse. Quìn potiùs ingenuè fateri minimè
erubescam, infœlicissimum meum Amyntam humi repere,
squallidum, et infirmum, dùm sibi non tam salutis spem
quærit, quàm exitij solatium. At qualiscúnque est colonus iste,
[π3ᵛ] generosissime Noelle, | eum tibi tam viuum, quàm demortuum
offero. Quid nî enìm et Fauni, et Panes aliquandò in Cæli-
colûm societatem et epulas admittantur? At quid nobis, fortè
inquies, cum querêlis? quis vnquam sapiens malorum amauit
nuncium? immò verò, quis nostrûm ità in Vlissem facilè se
commutauerit, vt Syrênum cantu et lenocinijs deliniri nolit?
aut quis tam ἀπαθής, vt lubenti et exporrecta aure non ex-
cipiat

     Quale suo recinit funere carmen olor?

Eo autem confidentiori animo istas tibi Querelas dicaui, partìm, quòd æruditissimis viris, quorum apud me authoritas
plurimum valere debet, satis probatæ fuerint: partìm, quià te
neminem inuêni digniorem qui eas à maleuolorum morsibus
tueretur: præsertìm verò, quià dilexi te, quo die cognoui
meque à te diligi iam diù in votis habui. Nam quî obliuisci
queam tam perbenigni aspectus, tam suauissimi sermonis,
[π4] miræque | humanitatis tuæ? Sed nolo tibi nimio verborum am-
bitu hìc molestus esse: nè aut Musæ lachrymis suis mendicare
stipem, aut à grauioribus te negocijs nimiùm interpellare
videantur. Deum itáque Optimum Maximum enixissimè precor, et assiduè precabor, nè vnquam aut meritis tuis gloriam,
aut virtuti fortunam deesse patiatur. Vale, vir Generosissime,
et quantulumcúnque me in clientêlis tuis numerato.

mentioned these writers, that I am so conceited and insolent as to dare to think that anyone should compare in any way my Complaints with Homer's *Batrachomyomachia*, or my Shepherd with Maro's Gnat, or my Phyllis with Petrarch's Laura. Rather I do not blush to confess, frankly, that my miserable Amyntas crawls on the ground, unadorned and weak, looking not for hope of safety, but rather for the solace of death. But whatever sort this rustic is, noble Noel, I offer him to you both living and dead. For why shouldn't the Fauns and Pans sometimes be admitted to the company and feasts of the gods? But what, you may ask perhaps, have we to do with complaints? What sane person has ever liked a harbinger of evil? But, on the other hand, who of us would change places with Ulysses and not want to be soothed by the singing and allurements of the Syrens? Or who so apathetic that he would not perk up his ear at

The song of the dying swan?

And in this rather confident frame of mind I have dedicated these complaints to you, partly because they were approved by learned men, whose authority ought to have great weight with me: partly because I found no one worthier than you to protect them from the carping of ill-wishers: and especially because I have esteemed you and kept you in my prayers ever since I learned that you esteemed me. For how could I forget such a kindly appearance, such pleasant speech and marvelous refinement as yours? But I do not want to trouble you here with too great a parade of words: lest my Muse should seem to beg a gift from your tears or to disturb you too much from more important business. And so I earnestly pray and continually will pray to God the Father Almighty that He never suffer your merits to lack glory or your ability, success. Farewell, noble gentleman, number me, however insignificantly, among your clients.

Ad Lectorem.

Nil opus est leuibus præludia texere nugis;
Si placeant, relegas: ni placeant, releges.

To the Reader

It isn't necessary to compose introductions to light trifles:
If you like it, peruse it: if not, refuse it.

Facsimile of device preceding the text in Watson's *Amyntas*. Original,
diameter 2.5″. Courtesy of the British Museum.

THE
Lamentations of Amyn-
tas for the death of Phillis, para-
phrastically translated out of Latine in-
to English Hexameters by
Abraham Fraunce.

LONDON
Printed by Iohn Wolfe, for Thomas Newman,
and Thomas Gubbin. *Anno Dom.* 1 5 8 7.

Facsimile of the title page of the 1587 edition of *The Lamentations of Amyntas.* Original, 6⅛″ × 4⅛″. Courtesy of the Bodleian Library.

[7]

To the Right Honourable,

*MIne afflicted mind and crased bodie, together with other ex-
ternall calamities haue wrought such sorowfull and lamentable
effects in me, that for this whole yeare I haue wholy giuen ouer
my selfe to mournfull meditations. Among others, Amintas is*

5 *one, which being first prepared for one or two, was afterward
by the meanes of a few, made common to manie, and so piti-
fully disfigured by the boistrous handling of vnskilfull pen men,
that he was like to haue come abroad so vnlike himselfe, as that
his own Phillis would neuer haue taken him for Amintas.*

10 *Which vtter vndoing of our poore shepeheard, I knew not well
otherwise how to preuent, but by repairing his ragged attire, to
let him passe for a time vnder your honourable protection. As
for his foes, they either generallie mislike this vnusuall kind of
verse, or els they fancie not my peculier trauaile. For the first, I*

15 *neuer heard better argument of them then this, such an one
hath done but ill, therefore no man can doe well, which reason
is much like their own rimes, in condemning the art, for the
fault of some artificers. Now for the second sort of reprehenders
who think well of the thing, but not of my labour therein, mine*

20 *answere is at hand. If there were anie penaltie appointed for
him that would not reade, he might well complaine of me that*
[¶2ᵛ] *publish it to be read. | But if it be in euerie mans choise to read
it, or not to reade, why then not in mine also to publish or not
to publish it? He that will, let him see and reade; he that will*

25 *neither reade nor see, is neither bound to see nor read. He that
taketh no delight in reading, let him thinke that among so
manie men so diuersly affected, there may be some found of a*

1 MIne] MY B C E; *omit* D—*see appendix*

15 an one] a one B C E

22–23 But . . . to reade] *omit* C E

23–24 or not to publish] *omit* C E

{ *8* }

*contrarie humor. If anie begin to read, when he beginneth to
take no delight, let him leaue of and goe no further. If he folow
on in reading without pleasure, let him neither blame me that did*   30
*what I could, nor be angrie with the thing which hath no sense,
but reprehend himselfe who would continue in reading without
any pleasure taking.*

Your honours
most affectionat.
Abraham Fraunce.

Amyntæ

QVERELA PRIMA.

Phyllida formoso raptam sub flore iuuentæ
Assiduo gemitu tristis lugebat Amyntas,
Mentis inops, plenus curæ, lachrymosus Amyntas,
Peruigili planctu syluas, montésque, lacúsque,
5 Speluncas, ripas, ventos, aurámque fatigans.
Ast vbi nequicquam se perfudisse videbat
Pallida iam nimiùm lachrymis manantibus ora,
Vlla nec inuênit miseri solatia luctus,
Tandem se Thamesis raucas conuertit ad vndas,
10 Et sic illachrymans affatur labile flumen.
    Audi nympha graues, audi pia nympha querelas,
Et tecum sinito cognati regna subire
Oceani, totum qui fluctibus alluit orbem.
Ille meos questus per inania littora secum
15 Deferet, vt nostræ sit tellus inscia flammæ
Nulla, meósque ignes calidæ testentur arenæ.
Forsan et ipse pater Ponti Tritona canorum
Cærulea concha passim spirare iubebit
Quos patior Siculis grauiores ignibus æstus.
20 Sic omnes præcone Deo vulgata per oras
Fama mei miseri, fama infœlicis Amyntæ
Tartareum per aquas tandem penetrabit Auernum,
Elysíjque domos lætas, lucósque subintrans,
[A1ᵛ] Occurret nimiùm dilectæ Phyllidos vmbræ,

16 testentur] testentnr 85

[Amyntas]

THE FIRST LAMENTATION.

IN flowre of young yeares fayre Phillis lately departing,
With teares continual was daily bewayld of Amyntas,
  halfe mad Amyntas, careful Amintas, mournful Amintas.
Whose mourning al night, al day, did weary the mountains,
Wearie the woods, and wyndes, and caues, and weary the   5
  fountains.
But when he saw in vaine his cheekes with teares to be watred,
  cheeks al pale and wan, yet could not finde any comfort,
  comfortles then he turns at length his watery countnance
Vnto the shril waters of Thames, and there he beginneth:
  Here, O nimph, these plaints, here, O good nimph, my be-   10
  wailings,
And conuey them downe to thy kinsmans watery kingdome,
Down to the world washing main sea with speedy reflowing:
Worldwashing main-sea wil then conuey to the worlds end
This grieuous mourning, by the shore, by the sands, by the
  desert,
Desert, sands, and shore which witnes were to my mourning.   15
  And great God Neptune perchaunce, his mightily thun-
  dring
Triton, wil commaund to recount what I feele, what I suffer,
Raging heate of loue, passing outragius Ætna.
  So th'infamous fame of wretched louer Amyntas,
Blown from th'east to the weast, by the sounding trump of a   20
  Triton,
Through deepe seas passing, at length may pearce to Auernus,
And fyelds Elysian where blessed souls be abyding.
And there meete Phillis, sweete soule of Phillis among them,

1–12 *altered in D—see appendix*
14 desert, A–E] desert. *faults escaped*
15 which witnes were] fit witnesses vnto D
18 outragius *faults escaped*] outragious A

25 Phyllidos, æternum quam flebo misellus Amyntas.
    O ego quàm fœlix tenera cum virgine Pastor.
    Quàm vixi verè fœlix dum fata sinebant.
    Sæpè, calore suo ne torrida læderet æstas,
    Sedimus vnanimes patulæ sub tegmine fagi,
30 Alter in alterius charis amplexibus hærens,
    Alter in alterius defixus lumina vultu,
    Ambo cantantes, autores carminis ambo,
    Ambo blandisonis miscentes oscula dictis.
    Eius et interdum tangebam mollia colla,
35 Colla nitore suo niueis æquanda ligustris,
    Dum nostro suspensa sinu, rubicundula risu
    Leni perplacuit, vel dum tractabat eburno
    Pollice quas habui sparsas lanugine mâlas.
    Forsan et ausus eram teretes quandóque papillas
40 Indigna mulcere manu, placidéque mouere.
    O mihi tum verni perdulces temporis horas,
    Fœlicésque dies, dum sydera læta micabant.
    At nunc (heu) quantus duris dolor ossibus ardet,
    Postquàm deseruit miserum me Phyllis Amyntam?
45 Nulla dies oritur nostri non conscia luctus,
    Et nox quamtumuis lasso fert nulla quietem:
    Luce mihi media, noctû mihi Phyllis oberrat.
      Nunc si quando feris Aquilonibus intonat æther,
    Et vaga tempestas nymbo delapsa fragoso
[A2] Meque, meúmque pecus viridi de gramine cogit
    Currere sub syluas, platanósque subire comantes,
    Phyllis abest, Phyllis nostræ solatia vitæ,
    Cui toties Veneris puerum, Venerémque canebam,
    Et lætas Charites, et Faunos, et Satyriscos:
55 Nec non visus eram socios superare canendo,
    Quotquot in his mecum pecoris sedêre magistri
    Vallibus: Heu, solus cui iam cantabit Amyntas?

Sweete soule of Phillis, stil, stil, to be mournd of Amyntas,
  O what a life did I leade, what a blessed life did I leade   *25*
    then,
Happy shepheard with a louing lasse, while destiny suffred?
Vnder a beech many times wee sate most sweetely together,
Vnder a broade beech tree that sunbeames might not anoy vs,
Either in others armes, stil looking either on other:
Both, many rimes singing, and verses both many making,   *30*
And both so many woords with kisses so many mingling.
Sometimes her white neck, as white as milk, was I tutching,
Sometimes her pretty paps, and breast was I bold to be fingring, [A1ᵛ]
Whil'st Phillis smyling and blushing hangd by my bosome,
And these cheekes of mine did stroke with her yuory fingers,   *35*
these cheekes with yong heare like soft downe all to bee
    smeared.
O ioyful spring time with pleasure wished abounding,
O those blessed dayes while good lucke shyn'd fro the heauens,
But since Phillis, alas, did leaue most cursed Amyntas,
Pains haue plagued, alas, both flesh and bones of Amintas,   *40*
No day riseth, alas, but it heares these grones of Amintas,
No night commeth, alas, that brings any rest to Amintas,
Night and day thus, alas, stil Phillis troubleth Amintas.
   Now if northern blasts should sound their feareful alarum,
And boistrous tempests, come thundring down fro the   *45*
    heauens,
So that I were compeld with sheepe and kidds fro the pastures
Down to the broadbrancht trees and thick set groues to be
    skudding,
There to remain for a while, and al for feare of a scowring,
Phillis then do I want, then my sweete Phillis is absent,
Phillis then do I want: whose wont was then to be harckning   *50*
Al that I could of loue, and goddes louely, remember:
Songs of lusty satyrs, and Fauni friends to the mountains,
And cheerefull Charites: such songs, as none but I onely,
Onely Amintas made, for none compar'd with Amintas:
   But now, Phillis I want, and who shal now bee my Phillis?   *55*

34 blushing *faults escaped*] bushing A
36 *omit* D   38 while] whilst B C D E
37 pleasure] pleasures B C D E   51 and goddes] or goddesse D

Phyllida si laudo, fors laudant Phyllida syluæ,
Phyllidáque abruptis repetit de collibus Eccho,
60　Mœroríque meo faciunt ludibria venti,
Ingemit et mecum dimissis crinibus arbos,
Et tacitò queritur mutato terra colore.
Sed rerum hac facie casus mihi crescit acerbus,
Dum solis oculi curis pascuntur, et aures.
65　　I tenerum pecus, et quondam mea cura, Capellæ,
Quærite nunc alibi vescas in pabula frondes,
Herbosas peragrate vias custode relicto, et
Me sine sub tectum, cùm venerit Hesperus, ite.
Vos aliquis pascet miserans, stabulísque reponet,
70　Solus ego dum flebo meam, vestrámque puellam
Phyllida, nam vestri curam quoque Phyllis habebat.
Solus ego degam duris in montibus æuum,
Tristes speluncas habitans, latebrásque ferarum,
Humanos quà nulla solet perducere gressus
75　Semita: Vel nemorum mœrens vmbracula quæram,
[A2ᵛ]　Exosus Phœbi radios, et lumina noctis:
Vt mihi taxicoléque stryges, coruúsque sinister,
Funereúsque canat feralia carmina bubo.
Illic hisce oculis lachrymarum copia tanta

The first Lamentation

Who shall marke what I sing, what I say, forsaken Amintas?
If that I praise Phillis, these hills giue praise to my Phillis,
And Phillis, Phillis, from rocks with an Eccho, reboundeth,
Thus by the whistling windes my mourning's made but a
    iesting.
If that I grone, these trees with bending, yeeld many gron-   60
    ings:
And very ground for griefe shews her complexion altred:
So this ground, these trees, these rocks, and Eccho resound-
    ing,
All that I heare, that I see, giues fresh increase to my sorrow.
    Go poore sheepe and kidds, sometimes the delyte of Amin-
    tas,
Seeke now somewhere else both gras and boughs to refresh   65
    you,
Make your way by the fields, and neuer looke for Amintas,
Lodge your selues at night, and neuer looke for Amintas.
Some pitiful goodman wil take compassion on you,
And feede you wandring, and bring you home by the euning.
    And I alone, yeelding due mourning vnto my Phillis,   70
Phillis mine and yours (for you also shee regarded)   [A2]
Ile now wander alone, stil alone, by the rocks, by the moun-
    tains,
Dwelling in darke dens by the wilde beasts only frequented,
Where no path for man, where no man's seene to bee passing:
Or to the woods Ile goe, so darke with broadshadoe   75
    braunches,
That no Sunne by the day, no starre by the night do anoy
    mee,
And that I heare no voice, but Goblins horrible outcries,
Owles baleful scrikings, and crowes vnlucky resoundings.
There shall these myne eyes be resolud in watery fountains:

59 mourning's B C E] mournings, A; D *omits line*

64–69 *omit* D, *substitute* Let those happy shepherds keepe company
fryendly togeather,

65 somewhere] fomewhere A

71 *omit* D   76 anoy] behould D

73 in] in the C E   78 vnlucky] vulucky A

80 Effluet, vt currant liquidæ de fletibus vndæ
Per virides campos, vicináque pascua circum.
Illíc verba querar sensus motura ferarum,
Quæque suis rigidas soluant radicibus ornos,
Panthêras faciant cicures, et mollia saxa.
85 Sin oculos somno sit declinare necesse,
In gelida prostratus humo languentia membra,
Tantillum stertam, sed nullo cespite fultus,
Nec superingesto ramorum pondere tectus:
Horrida vt incautum læthali vipera morsu
90 Enecet, et Stygias mea mens delata per vndas
Incolat Elysios campos cum Phyllidis vmbra.
Intereà vos, ô, Pastores candida turba,
Atque hæc qui colitis celeberrima rura Coloni,
(Pernouistis enim, et, nisi fallor, amatis Amyntam)
95 Blanditias Veneris me me monitore cauete,
Et calamos eius teneri, sed fortis alumni.
Illa suis facibus mea torruit, iste sagittis
Pectora percussit: quid sæuius igne, quid arcu?
Heu miseram sortem nimis infœlicis Amyntæ.

A　　**QVERELA SECVNDA.**

Cæruleæ Thamesis cum propter amœna fluenta
Plurima conquestus surdas clamasset ad vndas,
Flebilibúsque diem totum, noctísque tenêbras
Lamentis illic miser insumpsisset Amyntas,
5 Aurea quamprimum roseos Aurora capillos

83 rigidas] ragidas 85.

There shall these fountains flow ouer along by the pastures: 80
There wil I make such plaints, as beasts shal mourn by my
    playnings,
Such plaints, as strong trees shal rent and riue fro the rooting,
Make wylde Panthers tame, and mollify lastly the flintstone.
And if I needs must sleepe, I'le take but a nap by my sleeping,
On bare and cold ground, these lims al weary reposing: 85
No greene turfe to my head, shal stand in steede of a pillow,
No bowes or braunches geeue cou'ring vnto my carkas,
That some foule serpent may speedily giue me my deaths
    wound:
That this poore soule may from flesh and bloud be released,
And passing stygian waters, may come to the faire fields,   90
Elysian faire fields, and daily resort to my Phillis.
    Meane while, friendly shepheards and plowmen, mark
    what I tel you,
Marke what I say (for I think you knew and loued Amintas.)
Disdaine daintie Venus, give no ground vnto the blind boy,
Yong boy, but strong boy: take heede, take heed by Amintas.   95
Th'one with a fire hath burnt, and th'other pearst with an
    arrow
Flesh, and bones, and bloud: whats worse then a fire, then an
    arrow?
    O bitter fortune of too too wretched Amintas.

THE SECOND LAMENTATION. [A2ᵛ]

WHen by the pleasant streams of Thames poore caitif Amin-
    tas
Had to the dull waters his grief thus vainly reuealed,
Spending al that day and night in vainly reuealing,
As soone as morning her shining heares fro the mountains

84 sleepe, C D E] sleepe. A B
93 *omit* D
94 daintie] dame E blind] yong D
97 Flesh, and bones, and bloud] Flesh and blood and bones D
1–5 *omit* D—*see appendix*
2 his] of E   3 B C D E *omit line*

Ostendit, bigísque omni vaga sydera cælo
Dispulit, ille, sui cruciant quem semper amores,
Infœlix pastor iam nudas gramine ripas
Deseruit, curuóque pedo munitus, in altos
10   Ascendit colles, sed lentè et passibus ægris;
Lanigerósque greges unà, tenerásque capellas,
Et molles hœdos meliora ad pabula duxit:
Inque via secum sic est affatus euntes.
   Quàm vereor, Pecudes, nè, me dum tristis amantem
15   Cura tenet, nostros et vos ploretis amores.
Cur non balatis, cur non saltatis vt olim?
Quíd pratis agni, Baccho quíd parcitis hœdi?
Phyllida qui deflet, num vos defletis Amyntam?
Et pecori nocet vnus amor, pecorísque magistro?
20   Heu, quantæ sortes miseris mortalibus instant?
   Agnosco penitus quæ vobis causa querelæ
Surgat, et infandos mecum sufferre dolores.
Phyllis enim vobis prima sub nocte, Capellæ,
Vbera pressabat referentibus vbera plena.
25   Sæpè etiam vobis ludentibus illa tenellos
[A3ᵛ] Admouit flores, quos insuper accumbebat:
Exustásque siti flagranti sub Canis astro
Ad murmur salientis aquæ ducebat amicè,
Me placidum gelida somnum capiente sub vmbra.
30   Vosque meæ charæ, mea cura secunda, Bidentes,
Vos mecum fluuio Phyllis quandòque salûbri
Sordidulas mersare solet, purgatáque terga
Tondêre: in placidos tum saltus reddere lætas,

Had shewn forth, and dryu'n al star-light quite fro the   5
    heauens,
Then that vnhappy shepheard stil plag'd with vnhappily
    louing,
Left those barren banks and waters no pity taking,
And on a crookt sheephooke his lims all weary reposing,
Climed a loft to the hills, but, alas, very faintily clymed,
Kiddes, and goats, and sheepe driuing, goodman, to the   10
    mountains,
For sheepe, goats, and kidds with pastures better abounding,
Then by the way thus he spake, to the sheep, to the goats,
    to the yong kidds.
  O poore flock, it seems you feele these pangs of a louer,
And mourne thus to behold your mournful maister Amyntas.
Your wont was, some part to be bleating, some to be skipping,   15
Some with bended browes and horned pates to be butting,
Sheepe to be gnapping grasse, and goats to the vines to be
    climing.
But now no such thing, but now no lust to be liuely,
Sheepe and seelly sheepheard with lucklesse loue bee besotted,
You for Amintas mourne, for Phillis mourneth Amyntas,   20
O with what miseries poore mortal men be molested?
  Now do I know right wel what makes you thus to be
    mourning,
Thus to be tyred, thus to be quailed, thus to be drooping:
Phillis while she remaynd, milkt my goates euer at euning,
Goats that brought home duggs stretcht with milk euer at   25
    euning.
Phillis brought them flowres, and them brought vnto the
    welsprings,
When dogdayes raigned, when fields were al to be scorched,
Whilst that I lay sleeping in cooling shade to refresh mee.
  Phillis againe was woont with Amyntas, sheepe to be
    washing,
Phillis againe was wont my sheepe thus washt to be shearing,   30
Then to the sweete pastures my sheepe thus shorne to be
    driuing,

11 For B C D E] for A
22 mourning, A] mourning. A'   31 Then] And C D E

[19]

Emissáque lupos vulpésque arcere Lycisca,
35 Interdúmque domi tutis includere septis,
Aspera ne sævis Aquilonibus aura noceret
Mollibus, aut glacies, et atrocis frigora brumæ;
Vos adeò Phyllis, adeò me Phyllis amabat,
Phyllis erat vobis custos, mihi Phyllis amica.
40   Attamen ô blandum pecus, omnem ponite luctum,
Nostra nec aspicite illætis obtutibus ora
In fontes resoluta nouos, neque flentis amarè
Auribus arrectis mœstos haurite susurros,
Nec mea septeno quod canna foramine stridet
45 Insuetum querulúmque melos. Procul ite magistro,
Et facili saltu pictos percurrite campos,
Herbosúmque nemus lasciuo carpite morsu,
Et teneras vites: cursu sed abite citato,
Si venit impositus tardo Silenus asello.
50 Phyllidis exequias me me permittite solum
Et dulces cineres misera cantare querela:
[A4] "Qualis vbi longo mœrore Caïstrius ales
"Confectus, senióque graui, sua sentit adesse
"Funera, solus agens per frigida flumina cursum,
55 "In ripa tandem, graciles intérque genistas
"Considet, ac serò modulatus flebile carmen,
"Cum cantu vitam liquidas exhâlat in auras.
    Heu quò me vertam sine te mea vita secunda?
Quid sine te facient syluæ, quid prata, quid agri?
60 Ipsa Pales agros, ex quo te fata tulerunt,

45 insuetum] iusuetum 85.

The second Lamentation

And from fox and woolfe my sheepe thus dryu'n to bee keep-
    ing
With watchfull bawling and strength of lustie Lycisca,
And in folds and coates my flocke thus kept, to be closing: [A3]
Least by the Northern winds my sheepe might chance to be   35
    pinched
Least by the frost or snow my kids might chance to be
    grieued.
Phillis lou'd you so, so Phillis loued Amintas,
Phillis a guide of yours, and Phillis a friend of Amintas.
But sweete sheepe, sweete goates, spare not to be liuelie, for
    all this,
Looke not vpon my weeping face so sadly, for all this,   40
Harken not to my plaints and songs all heauie, for all this,
Harken not to my pipe, my pipe vnluckie, for all this.
But sweete sheepe, sweete goates, leaue of your maister
    Amintas,
Leape and skip by the flowring fields, and leaue of Amintas,
Climbe to the vines and tender trees, and leaue of Amintas,   45
Climbe to the vines, but runne for life, for feare of a mis-
    chiefe,
When th'old Silenus with his Asse comes lasilie trotting,
Let me alone, me alone lament and mourne my beloued,
Let me alone celebrate her death by my teares, by my mourn-
    ing:
    Like to the siluer swan, who seeing death to be comming,   50
Wandreth alone for a while through streames of louelie
    Caïster,
Then to the flowring bankes all faint at length he repaireth,
Singing there, sweet bird his dying song to Caïster,
Geuing there, sweet bird, his last farewell to Caïster,
Yeelding vp, sweete bird, his breath and song to Caïster.   55
    How can Amintas liue, when Phillis leaueth Amintas?
What for fieldes, for woods, for medowes careth Amintas,
Medowes, woods, and fieldes if my sweete Phillis abandon?
    Mightie Pales fro the fieldes, fro the medowes learned
    Apollo,

32 And] Then C D E   37 loued *faults escaped*] lou'd A
33 *omit* C D E   46 but] And E

Et Faunus syluas, et prata relinquit Apollo:
Dulcia non oculis, non auribus vlla feruntur.
Sin redeas mea Phylli meis permota querelis,
Gramine prata, nemus folijs, et floribus agri
65   Turgebunt, miserísque ferent optata colonis;
Nempè suos fœcunda Pales redamabit agellos,
Et Faunus syluas, et pascua lætus Apollo:
Tristia non oculis, non auribus vlla ferentur.
    Ergò istas iterum (si fas) remeato sub auras,
70   Deseritóque locus lætos, et amœna vireta
Fortunatorum nemorum, mánésque tremendos
Vince tuis oculis, quibus aurea sydera vincis.
Et blando sermone, cheli qui dulcior ipsa
Threicei Vatis, Furias, Plutonáque toruum
75   Placato, Stygijque canis compesce furorem:
Orphea nam cantu superas, pietate Sybillam.
Dulcis amica redi, propera mea dulcis amica,
[A4ᵛ] Nî redeas properè fletu tabescet Amyntas.
    Te per ego has lachrymas, et per candentia nostro
80   Quæ sinuata soles collo dare brachia circum,
Perque datam totiés nobis dextrámque fidémque,
Perque labella meis totiés coniuncta labellis,
Per nostros cantus per promissos Hymenæos,
Per quicquid de te merui, fuit aut tibi quicquam
85   Dulce meum, miserere mei pereuntis, et istis
Oro (si quis adhuc precibus locus) exime curis.
Aut saltem lachrymis crudelia numina Parcas
Flecte tuis, ne me solum sine te mea Phylli,
Vlteriúsque sinant lento marcessere luctu.

The second Lamentation

Faunus went fro the woods, when Phillis went from Amintas,   60
No good sight to my eyes, no good sound came to my hearing.
But let Phillis againe come backe, and stay with Amintas,
Then shall woods with leaues, and fields with flowers be
    abounding,
Medowes with greene grasse to the poore mans dailie reioic-
    ing,
Mightie Pales to the fields, to the medowes learned Apollo,   65
Faunus comes to the woods, if Phillis come to Amintas,
No bad sight to my eyes, no bad sound comes to my hearing.
    Come then, good Phillis, come back, if destinie suffer,
Leaue those blessed bowers of soules alreadie departed,
Let those sparkling eyes most like to the fire, to the Christall,   70
Ouercome those hags and fiends of fearful Auernus.
Which haue ouercome those stars of chearful Olympus.   [A3ᵛ]
And by thy speech more sweet then songs of Thracian Or-
    pheus,
Pacify th'infernall furies, please Pluto the grim god,
Stay that bawling curre, that three throate horrible helhound,   75
For vertue, for voice, th'art like to Sibilla, to Orpheus.
    Sweet hart, come, to thy friend, to thy friend come speede-
    lie sweethart.
Speedelie come, least grief consume forsaken Amintas.
Phillis, I pray thee returne, if prayers may be regarded,
By these teares of mine, from cheekes aie rueful abounding,   80
By those armes of thine, which somtimes clasped Amintas,
By lips thine and mine, ioined most sweetly together,
By faith, hands, and hart with true sinceritie pledged,
By songs, by wedding with great solemnitie vowed,
By iests, and good turns, by pleasures all I beseech thee,   85
Helpe and succor, alas, thy forlorne louer Amintas.
Or by thy teares intreat those nimphs of destenie fatall,
No pitie taking nimphs intreat, that I liue not alone thus,
Pind thus away with griefe, suffring vnspeakable anguish,
But let death, let death, come spedelie giue me my pasport,   90

63 with leaues] and leaues E   71 fearful *faults escaped*] fearefull A
66 Faunus comes] come C'   75 throate *faults escaped*] throt A
69 of] and E soules] foules A   87–88 those nimphs . . . intreat] *omit* C E

[*23*]

90 Si moriar, syluas Erebi, sedésque beatas
Inueniam, tecúmque fruar fœlicibus horis.
Officijs ibi te vincam, tu me quoque vinces,
Florea serta tuo capiti mea dextera texet,
Florea serta meo capiti tua dextera texet,
95 Ambóque sub viridi myrto repetemus amores,
Quos olim parili versu cantauimus ambo.
    Sed quorsum leuibus nequicquam talia ventis
Conqueror infœlix, ac si suspiria mixta
Cum lachrymis fixum possint diuertere fatum?
100   Inde domum lugens sub nocte oriente redibat.

[A5]   *QVERELA TERTIA.*

Tertia iamque dies aderat post cruda puellæ
Funera, cùm grauibus curis oppressus Amyntas
Exêmit stabulis hœdos, et ouilia septis,
Ac iuga vicini collis frondosa petiuit.
5 Quà raptam pecudes inter dum deflet amicam,
Votáque multa ædit singultibus interrupta
Ventosis, mollésque vago diuerberat auras
Mugitu, sonitus extremos flebilis Eccho
Non repetit, memor ipsa sui, quo languet, amoris,
10 Sed pulchrum tacito Narcissum corde volutans
Soluitur in lachrymas, nectítque dolore dolorem,
Dumque cupit fari, linguam suspiria sistunt,
Impediúntque sonos, et vox in gutture pendet,
More nec assueto mœstum deludit amantem.
15 Talia questus erat Pastor, dum constitit illa,
Mutáque lugenti miserantem præbuit aurem.

So that I find faire fields, faire seats, faire groues by my dy-
    ing,
And in fields, in seats, in groues faire Phillis abiding.
There shal Phillis againe, in curtesie striue with Amintas.
There with Phillis againe, in curtesie striue shal Amintas,
There shall Phillis againe make garlands gay for Amintas,   95
There for Phillis againe, gay garlands make shal Amintas,
There shal Phillis againe be repeating songs with Amintas,
Which songs Phillis afore had made and song with Amintas.
  But what, alas, did I meane, to the whistling winds to be
    mourning?
As though mourning could restore what destenie taketh.   100
  Then to his house, ful sad, when night approcht, he re-
    torned.

THE THIRD LAMENTATION.   [A4]

ANd now since buriall of Phillis lcuely, the third day
At length appeared, when that most careful Amintas
Loost his kids fro the fold, and sheepe let forth fro the sheep-
    coats,
And to the neighbour hils full set with trees he resorted,
Where, as amidst his flocke, his lasse thus lost he bewaileth,   5
And makes fond wishes with deepe sighs interrupted,
And the relenting aire with his owtcries all to bebeateth;
Eccho could not now to the last words yeeld anie Eccho,
All opprest with loue, for her old loue still she remembred,
And she remembred still, that sweet Narcissus her old loue,   10
With teares all blubbred, with an inward anguish amased.
When she begins to resound, her sobs still stay the resound-
    ing,
When she begins her speech, her griefe still stoppeth her
    halfe speech,
With which her wont was with louers sweetlie to dallie.
  During these her dumps, thus againe complaineth Amintas,   15
During these his plaints, she with all compassion harkneth.

                  7 owtcries] outcrie C E
91 that] shal B C D E   8 words] woord D
101 his] the E   16 these his plaints] his complaynts D

Hei, quantum nobis indicit Cypria bellum?
Quales condit Amor faculas sub pectore nostro,
Vt tam longa dies nequeat producere pacem,
20 Nec cæcas fontes lachrymarum extinguere flammas?
Funditus (heu) perij, postquam malè cautus ocellis
Aspexi cupidis superantia labra corallum,
Sydereos oculos, spaciosáque tempora lætæ
Frontis, et aurata radiantes luce capillos,
25 Ac niueas candore genas, ostróque rubentes,
[A5ᵛ] Puráque mobilibus turgentia pectora venis,
Et quales digitos Tithoni blandula coniux
Vix habet, annosam dum texit pollice barbam.
Cætera quid memorem nullis intersita næuis
30 Membra? quid oblongo vestigia condita peplo?
Crebra quid Ambrosijs sermonibus oscula iuncta,
Iunctáque baseolis haud irrita verba pudicis
Sub lauro Phœbi, Venerísque sub arbore myrto?
Talia surripuit mihi gaudia fictilis vrna,
35 Quæ modo combustæ liuentia contegit ossa
Phillidis, heu nimiùm precioso pondere fœlix,
Et nimiùm fœlix tellus, quæ contegit vrnam.
Mundi delicias, ac primæ summa parentis
Munera Naturæ, nostrósque tenetis amores,
40 Et Solem ruris nostri, Nemorúmque Dianam,
Pastorúmque Palem, et virtutum dotibus amplis
Pandoram (sed erat vicijs exuta) secundam.
Heu nimiùm fœlix terra, et fœlicior vrna.
Tuque, ô, ter fœlix, tumulo quod crescis ab illo
45 Gramen, et in dulces tenerum caput exeris auras,
Molli mulcendum Zephyro, nullísque secandum

O what a warre is this with loue thus still to be striuing?
O what a wild fire's this conueid to my hart by the blind boy?
That neither long time can bring anie end to my striuing
Nor teares extinguish this wild fire thrown by the blind boy?　20
　Then then, alas, was I lost, ô then then, alas, was I vndone,
When the corall colored lips were by me greedelie vewed,
And eies like bright stars, and faire browes daintily smiling,
And cheareful forehead with gold wire al to bedecked,
And cheekes al white red, with snow and purple adorned,　25
And pure flesh swelling with quicke vaines speedilie mouing,
And such fine fingers, as were most like to the fingers
Of Tithonus wife, platting th'old beard of her husband.
　What shal I say to the rest? each part vnited in order,
Each part vnspotted, with long roabes couered each part.　30
What shal I say to the rest? manie kisses ioynd to the sweet
　words,
And manie words of weight in like sort ioind to the kisses,
Vnder a greene Laurell sitting, and vnder a myrtle,　[A4ᵛ]
Myrtle due to Venus, greene Laurell due to Apollo.
That litle earthen pot these ioyes hath now fro me snatched,　35
That litle earthen pot where Phillis bones be reserued,
O thrise happie the pot, where Phillis bones be reserued,
And thrise happie the ground, where this pot shall be re-
　serued.
Earth, and earthen pot, you haue the belou'd of Amintas,
Natures sweete deareling, and onelie delight to the whole　40
　world,
And sunne of this soile, of these woods onelie Diana,
Onelie Pales of seelie shepeheards, Pandora the goddes,
Excluding all faults, including onelie the goodnes,
O thrise happie the earth, but much more happie the earth
　pot.
　O thrise happie the grasse that growes on graue of a goddes,　45
And shooting vpward, displayes his top to the heauens.
Sweete blasts of Zephyrus shall make this grasse to be seeme-
　lie,

20 wild] omits C E　　　　　40 whole world] Countrey D
31 shal *faults escaped*] shall A　　47 Zephyrus *faults escaped*] Lephyrus A

Falcibus, et cuius folijs incumbere serpens
Horreat, afflatúque suo, tabóque nocere,
Aut plantis vrsus, cornu bos, vngue leæna,
50   Aut rostris volucres, aut gressu reptile quicquam,
Aut glacialis hyems, aut lunæ roscidus humor,
[A6] Aut Phœbi calor, aut igniti sydera cæli,
Aut fera tempestas, aut diræ fulminis alæ.
    Hinc armenta, precor, procul hinc arcete bubulci,
55   Vos quoque Pastores, procul hinc conducite turbas,
Nè pecus ignarum nostro lædatur amore,
Neù minuat taurus tumulatæ virginis ossa,
Dum pedibus calcat, vel cornu spargit arenam:
Hic locus hic sacer est, latet ipsa Phyllis in herba.
60   Huc properate mares teneri, cultæque puellæ,
Spargite monticulum sanctum lustralibus vndis,
Constructásque pyras fagis implete Sabæo
Thure, leuísque æther iucundo fragret odore:
Atque Arabis collecta manu date cynnama busto
65   Phyllidis, et miti casia, violísque et amomo,
Purpureísque rosis, pulchróque tegatur Acantho.
Vndíque tum sacras flammis accendite ceras,
Nudáque neglectis tundentes pectora palmis,
Aurea funereos ad sydera tollite cantus
70   Tristibus eulogijs plenos, et honore puellæ.
Vobiscum Satyríque leues, Fauníque bicornes,
Et simplex Dryadum, Charitúmque sacerrima turba
Haud intermissas fundet miseranda querelas.
    Intereà pollinctor ego mœstissimus atri
75   Funeris ad talos morientia lumina gestans,
Lassabo plangore nemus, mediósque per agros
Fletibus orta meis labentur flumina, magno

No Sithe shall touch it, no serpent craftelie lurking
With venymous breathing, or poison deadlie shall hurt it:
No Lionesse foule pawes, Beares foot, beastes horne shall   50
    abuse it,
No birds with pecking, no vermine filthie by creeping,
No winters hoare frost, no night dewes dangerus humor,
No rage of suns heat, no starres or power of heauens,
No boistrous tempest, no lightnings horrible outrage.
   Driue hence, good plowmen, driue hence your wearied   55
    oxen,
And you, friendlie shepeheards, kepe back your sheepe fro the
    graues grasse
Least your sheepe vnwares may chaunce by my loue to be
    harmed,
Least by the bulles rude rage her bones may chaunce to be
    bruised,
Whilst with foot and horne he the graues ground teareth
    asunder.
   Make hast you young men, make hast all you pretie   60
    damsels,
With sacred water this sacred place to besprinkle:
Burne Piles of beache trees, and then cast on the sabæan
Spice to the Piles burning, send sweet perfumes to the
    heauens,
Cinnamon, and Casia, violets, and loued Amomum,
Red colored roses, with Bearebreech cast ye together.   65
   And then on euerie side set tapers sacred in order,
And beate your bare brests with fists all wearie for anguish,
And sing sweet Epitaphes, lifting your voice to the heauens,
Sing soure sweete Epitaphes in death and prayse of a goddes.
Wanton fleshly Satyrs, and Fauni friends to the mountaines,   70
Nimphs addict to the trees, and in most gracius order   [B1]
Three graces ioining, shall beare you companie mourning.
   And I my selfe will dresse, embalme, and chest my beloued,
And folowing her coarse, (all pale and wan as a dead man,)
Wearie the woods with plaints, and make new streams by my   75
    weeping

49 venymous *faults escaped*] venomous A
73 embalme] enbalme C E

[29]

[A6ᵛ] Quæ neque contineant surgentes aggere ripæ,
Nec Canis Icarij torrentia sydera potent.
80 Mecum Parnassus, mecum lugebit Apollo,
Et Parcis infensa Venus pro Phyllide rapta.
Æternámque facem ponet, pictámque pharêtram
Improbus ille puer, qui me cum Phyllide iunxit,
Lachrymulísque suis tristes lenire querelas
85 Ipse paratus erit, licet vnica causa querelæ.
    Sed quorsum demens iterum pia funera canto
Phyllidis? infœlix quid seris nænia fletur
Lamentis? nostros (heu) ter lustrauit agellos,
Terque caput retulit subter Nereïdos vndas
90 Phœbus, et Antipodas totiès despexit ab axe,
Quòd busti fuerint solennia quæque peracta,
Clausáque puluereo solatia nostra sepulchro.
Attamen insano iuuat indulgere dolori,
Et lachrymas lachrymis, et curas addere curis,
95 Nulláque concedent mœrori tempora finem.
Heu nimias vires et sæua Cupidinis arma!
Non tantas rebar fore blandi vulneris iras,
Cùm iecur exussit primùm, viridésque medullas,
Cumque meum tenui traiecit arundine pectus.
100 Tale querens casulam repetit sub vespere pastor.

[A7]   *QVERELA QVARTA.*

Ter Phœbus mundo lucem, rebúsque colores
Abstulerat, claráque diem iam lampide quartum
Induxit, tumulo post condita virginis ossa,

Such streames as no banck shall barre, streams euer abound-
    ing,
Such streames as no drought shall drie, streames neuer
    abating.
With me Parnassus, with me shall mourne my Apollo,
And Venus, all chafed that destenie tooke my beloued.
    And that same vile boy that first did ioine me to Phillis,   80
His lamp shall laie downe, and painted quiuer abandon,
And with his owne pretie teares trickling, and sweetlie be-
    seeming,
Help me to mourn, althogh that he gaue first cause to my
    mourning.
    But what, alas, do I meane to repeat these funeral outcries.
Still to repeat these songs, and still too late to repeat them?   85
Thrise hath Phœbus now displaid his beames fro the moun-
    taines,
Thrise hath Phœbus now discended downe to the maine sea,
Since my beloud was dead, since our good companie parted,
Since Phillis buried, since all solemnities ended,
Since my delites, poore wretch, were all inclosd in a coffin,   90
Yet do I mourne here still, though no good coms by my
    mourning,
Adding tears to my tears, and sorrows vnto my sorrows,
And no stay to my tears, and no rest coms to my sorrows.
    O strong boy, strong bow, and O most dangerus arrow,
Now doe I find it a paine, which first did seeme but a pleasure,   95
Now doe I feele it a wound, which first did seeme but a
    smarting,
When strong boy, strong bow, shot first that dangerus arrow.
    Thus did Amintas mourne, and then came home by the
    sonset.

THE FOURTH LAMENTATION. [B1ᵛ]

THrise had shining sunne withdrawn his face fro the heauens,
And earth all darkned, since Phillis friendlie departed,
And when fourth day came, then againe true louer Amintas,

93 *omit* C E
94 and O most dangerus arrow] shot first that dangerous arrow C E

[*31*]

Querela quarta

Cum memor antiquæ flammæ lugubris Amyntas
5 Noluit arbuteis hœdos discludere caulis
More suo, et pastum notos tranare per amnes:
Aut per vicini nodosa cacumina montis.
Solus at incedens per agros, ad flumina tandem
Cognita procumbit, laticíque intentus ocellos
10 Hæret, inexpletum lachrymans, ac talia fatur.
   Me miserum, quid agam? quò nunc vestigia vertam
Infœlix pastor? cineres mânésque sepulti
Non mala percipiunt, neque fletus commouet Orcum.
Phyllis ibi nostrum iam dedignatur amorem,
15 Et Stygij sequitur crudelia iussa tyranni,
Frangere docta fidem, furuúmque subire cubile.
Naiades, ô, quæso, si dicere forte potestis,
Dicite si famulas inter Iunonis Auernæ
Molliculo ducit candentia pollice fila.
20 Nam vereor nullo ne sit reditura sub æuo.
   Aruorum, ô, pecorísque Deus Syluane, Deorum
Summe mihi, miseri cur non miserescis Amyntæ?
Cur non ad nostrum immortalia numina votum
Inflectis? tu namque potes cœlestibus ortus
25 Principijs. Ego te per quæ tibi sacra dicaui
[A7ᵛ] Plurima, perque tuos animos ergà Cyparissum
Formosum puerum, precor, vt pereuntis Amyntæ
Ad casus doleas, multo faciásque rogatu
Phyllida restitui nobis, aut fata seuera
30 Morte mihi imposita cunctantes demere curas.
   Tu verò tandem mihi quid scelerate Cupido
Consulis? exanimem cupienti visere fata
Vltima sunt tentanda mihi mortalibus ausis:
Nec moror hanc animam quocunque absumere læthe.
35 O crudelis Amor, tu nostri pectoris ignes
Aspicis, et tacito crescentes corde dolores,
Et plenos nymbis oculos, miserétque tuentem
(Heu) nostri miseret, scio, quamuis ipse tyranni

Mindful of old loue stil, tooke no ioy flock to be feeding,
But stil alone wandring, through fields, to the banks, to the   5
    waters,
Leaned his head on bank, and eyes cast down to the waters,
With teares incessant his cheeks full waterie washing.
    What now resteth, alas, to be doone of woful Amintas?
No sence, no knowledge in these vnsensible ashes,
In graue no feeling, in death ther's no pitie taking.   10
    Phillis makes but a iest, dead Phillis mocketh Amintas.
Phillis breaks her faith, and plaies with Pluto the black
    prince,
Pluto the black prince now enioies those ioies of Amintas.
    Speak on, good sweet nymphs, if you can tell anie tidings,
Whether among those trulls that wait on Queene of Auernus,   15
My Queene and Empres, my Phillis chaunce to be spinning?
Speake, for I feare, for I feare, shee'l neuer come to Amintas,
    And thou Syluanus, Siluanus god to the mountains,
And flocks on mountains, ô helpe most helples Amintas,
Helpe by thy selfe, by thy friends, thou god cause gods to   20
    be helping.
For my religion, for my deuotion help me,
For thine own boyes sake, for loue of sweet Cyparissus,
Either let Phillis be returned backe to Amintas,
Or let Amintas dye, that death may succor Amintas.
    And thou naughtie Cupid, yet say on, giue me thy coun-   25
    sail,
What shal I do, shal I dye? shal Amintas murder Amintas?
Dye then Amintas: death will bring Phillis to Amintas.
O hard harted loue, thou seest what I beare, what I suffer,
Hart with flames, and eyes with mournful water abounding,
Head with cares possest, and soule ful of horrible anguish,   30
This thou seest, and sure I do know, it greeus thee to see this,
Though they call thee tyrant, though so thou iustlie be called,

<hr/>

8 woful] wilfull E
10 taking] taken C E   17 feare, for] feare, I C E
13 Amintas. B C D E] Amintas, A   18 And thou Syluanus] Father
14 tell] shew D   Syluanus D god] good A–E
15 among] amongst C E   22 *omit* D

Nomen habes, crudo Busyride sæuior ipso.
40   Scilicet et nobis eadem stat causa querelæ:
Nam tua cum nostra infœlix impingit eundem
In scopulum puppis, dum vento lædimur vno.
Dum rapitur Phyllis, nobis fortuna duobus
Vna datur, similísque ambos iniuria torquet.
45   Chara tibi, mihi chara fuit formosula Phyllis:
Nempe erat imperij notissima gloria vestri,
Et ruris speculum, et solum solamen amantum:
Et mea sola salus erat, et mea sola voluptas,
Spes mea, vita mea, ac animæ pars altera Phyllis.
50   O quæ sufficiant ad iustas verba querelas?
    Tuque ingrata nimis Tellus, iam desine flores
[A8] Amplius, aut dulces nobis concedere fructus
Postquam discessit Phyllis, vestigia cuius
Mollia portasti toties, et amabile pondus
55   Corporis, egregium vultus mirata decorem;
Eructa patulis mugentia flamina venis,
Vt cæli facies ventorum turbine pulsa
Luctantes pluuias dimittat nubibus atris;
Talis enim tristi cum fletu conuenit humor.
60   Ingemina mecum luctus, tantósque dolores
Concipe nunc animo, quantos, cum turba scelesta
Anguipedes olim concussi fulmine sacro

Though thy nature passe Busiris beastlie behauiour: [B2]
For what makes me to mourne, may cause thee to yeeld to
    my mourning:
One rude rock, one wind, and one tempestuus outrage   35
Batters, breaks, and beats thy ship, my ship to the quick-
    sands.
Our harms are equal, thy shipwrack like to my shipwrack,
Loue did loue Phillis, Phillis was loud of Amintas,
Phillis loues dearling, Phillis dearling of Amintas,
Dearling, crowne, garland, hope, ioy, wealth, health of   40
    Amintas,
And what more shal I say? for I want words fit for Amintas.
    And thou churlish ground, now cease anie more to be
    fruitful,
Cease to be deckt with flowres, and all in greene to be man-
    tled,
Thy flowre is withered, my garland latlie decaied,
Phillis thine and mine with death vntimelie departed,   45
Whose sweet corps thou bar'st, whose footsteps in thee be
    printed,
And whose face thou didst admire for beawtie renowmed,
Belch out roaring blasts with gaping iawes, to the heauens,
That those roaring blasts may scoure by the skyes, by the
    heauens,
And foule struggling storms cast down fro the clouds, fro the   50
    heauens
For such foule weather will best agree with a mourner.
Howle and mourne thou earth, and roare with an horrible
    outcrie,
Howle as then thou didst, when mountains were to the moun-
    tains
Put, by thy cursed brood, to be clyming vp to Olympus,
When great flakes of fire came flashing down fro the   55
    heauens,

34 cause thee to yeeld B C D E] cause thee: yeeld A; cause to yeeld
faults escaped
  36 thy ... my] my ... thy D thy ship] *omit* C E
  37 shipwrack] shipwrack's D
  40 wealth, health] health, wealth D

Præcipites ruerent in te tua viscera nati,
Et cum defleres subiectum Pelion Ossæ.
65 Aut quales alto curas tum corde gerebat
Alma Ceres, quandò ludentem in vallibus Ætnæ
Filiolam rapuit furui prædator Auerni,
Nocte sub æterna sociare cubilia secum.
Immemor, ô, nimium Tellus, quæ Phyllidis vmbram
70 Non iniussa pijs lachrymis comitaris ad Orcum.
Tu tam cælesti si pondere digna fuisses,
Non ita prærapido nobis erepta fuisset
Sydere, nec mortis crudam perpessa sagittam
In teneris annis, et sub florente iuuenta.
75 O nimiùm crudele malis aspectibus astrum,
O misero nimiùm pastori noxia fata.
      Hei mihi quòd terræ subeat mutata figuram,
[A8ᵛ] Candida quæ dudum visa est, et amabilis ore
Purpureo, roseísque genis, collóque nitenti,
80 Diuiduísque comis, oculísque rotantibus ignes.
      O fœlix Tithone, thoros tua sole cadente
Assuetos repetit coniux, puerúmque relinquens
Æolium, vitreo recubat sub marmore tecum,
Amplexúque tenet barbam dignata senilem.
85 Sed mea dum Phyllis toto disiungitur Orco,
Candida nigra mihi fiunt, et dulcia amara,
Perque diem noctémque queror, madefactáque multo
Mollescit fletu limosi glarea ruris,
Et ferio clamore vias, et sydera planctu:
90 Qualis per frutices gelidis philomela sub vmbris,
E nido raptos variato carmine pullos
Deflet, agros implens mœsta lucósque querela.
Nec redijsse potest Phyllis: crudelia fata
Immersas Erebo mentes hoc lucis ab orbe
95 Detinet, ac nouiès Styx interfusa coërcet.

When thy crawling sons came tumbling down from Olympus.
   Howle as ladie Ceres did then, when prince of Auernus
Stole her daughter away from fields that ioyned on Ætna,
Vnto the dungeons dark, and dens of his hellish abiding.
Thou ground, forgetful what was by dutie required,   60
Shouldst send, vnbidden, with Phillis, teares to Auernus.
Her blessed burden thou wast vnworthie to carrie,
Therefore tender girle in flowring age she departed.
O frowning fortune, ô stars vnluckilie shining,
O cursed birth day of quite forsaken Amintas.   65
Phillis, alas, is changd, Phillis conuerted in ashes,
Whose pretie lips, necke, eyes, and haire so sweetlie beseem-
    ing,
Purple, snow, and fire, and gold wire seemd to resemble.
   Tithonus faire wife coms alwaies home by the sunset,
Euerie night coms home to that old Tithonus her husband,   70
Sweete Cephalus leauing, and graybeard hartily kissing: [B2ᵛ]
But my Phillis, alas, is gone as farre as Auernus,
Gone too farre to returne, and this tormenteth Amyntas.
White is blacke and sweete is sowre to the sence of Amyntas,
Night and day doe I weepe, and make ground moist by my   75
    weeping,
Mourne, lament, and howle, and powre forth plaints to the
    heauens.
So do the Nightingales in bushes thorny remayning
Sing many dolefull notes and tunes, sweet harmony making,
Their yong ones mourning, their yong ones daily bewailing.
   Phillis, alas, is gone, shee'le neuer come to Amyntas,   80
Never againe come backe, for death and destiny stay her,
Stay her among those groues, and darksome dens of Auernus,
Wher's no path to returne, no starting hole to be scaping,
Desteny, death, and Hell, and howling hydeus helhound,
Loathsome streams of stix, that ninetimes compas Auer-   85
    nus,

                   64 frowning B C D E] frowning, A

61 Phillis] Phills A   72 is gone as farre as] is gone, is gone to D
62 carrie] beare up D   84 howling hydeus] Cerberus horrible D

Nil igitur superest eius, nisi dulcis imago,
Et charum nomen nullis violabile sæclis.
   Inde domum sese retulit miserandus Amyntas.

     QVERELA QVINTA.

Iamque iterum, charæ post funera ritè peracta
Phillidis, Oceani fuluum caput extulit vndis
Phœbus, et Eoo pellebat sydere noctem,
Ac lucem quintam misero præbebat Amyntæ.
5   Ille sed extinctæ crudelia fata puellæ
Ingemuit, mœsto curas sub pectore versans
Assiduas; Neque iam tenerum curabat ouile
Amplius, aut molles imponere collibus hœdos:
Sed solitum munus, lucémque perosus adortam,
10 Solus in antiqui nemoris se contulit vmbras.
Quà querula flentes hyacinthos voce fatigans,
Vesanis resonas plangoribus impulit auras,
Et gemitu ventos augens, et fletibus amnes,
Nequicquam vano mœrens indulsit amori;
15 "Qualis amans turtur, sociæ post fata columbæ
"(Rusticus annosa quam pastor ab arbore fundo
"Incautam nimis, aut calamo deiecit acuto)
"Incolit obscuras, exosus lumina, syluas,
"Feralémque, Iouis quam lambit flamma, cupressum,
20 "Aut quam tristis hyems afflauit turbine nigro,
"Solus init, putríque suos in vimine luctus
"Exprimit, et viduo rorem diffundit ocello,
"Dum gemitu arescens, victúsque doloribus, alto
"Culmine languenti in terram delabitur ala,

Stay her amongst those hags in dungeons ougly for euer.
Only the name and fame, and her most happy remembrance
still shal abide, shal liue, shal florish freely for euer.
Thus did Amyntas speake, and then came feyntily home-
ward.

THE FYFTH LAMENTATION. [B3]

SInce Phillis buriall with due celebration ended,
Phœbus againe aduanct his blasing face fro the maynesea
And with morning Star dispelling night fro the heauens
Quickly the fifth time brought broad day light vnto Amyntas:
But yet Phillis in heart, in mind, and soule of Amyntas   5
Stil did abyde, and stil was Phillis mournd of Amyntas.
No care of driuing his goats and kidds to the mountains,
No care of folowing his sheepe and lambs to the pastures,
But dailight loathing, and dayes worke wonted abhorring,
Straight to the woods doth he walke, in no mans company   10
   walking,
Where hee the weeping flowre making al weary by weeping,
Vntuned speeches cast out, and desperat outcries,
Where, with sobs to the windes, with teares increase to the
   waters
Stil did he giue, and stil vayne loue most vaynly bewayled.
As louing Turtle seeing his lately beloued   15
Turtle-doue thrown downe from tree, with a stone, with an
   arrow,
Can not abide sun-beames, but flies fro the fields, fro the
   meddows,
Vnto the darkest woods, and there his desolat harbor
Makes in a Cypres tree, with lightning all to be scortched,
Or with Winters rage and blacke storms fowly defaced: 20
Where on a rotten bow his lyms all heauy reposing,
Stil doth he grone for griefe, stil mourne for his onely beloued,
Then consum'd with grieuous pangs, and weary with anguish,
Down to the ground doth he fal with fainting wings fro the
   barebow,

89 speake] plaine D
7 goats and kidds] kydds and goats D
13 sobs] sighes D

15 beloued B C D E] beloued. A;
faults escaped describes "a comma
too much," *in fact, a period*

25   "Ac tremulas turpi miscens cum puluere plumas,
[B1ᵛ] "Mollia transadigit falcato pectora rostro,
    "Fundit et insonti tristem cum sanguine vitam.
    Talia verba dolor misero suffecit Amyntæ.
      Heu, quàm sæua mihi nocuere Cupidinis arma,
30   Æternúmque meo cordi constantiùs hærent,
    "Quàm trunco cortex, vlmo quàm vitis agresti,
    "Quàm muris hederæ, quàm stagnis muscus aquosis?
    Heu crudelis Amor, quid non mortalia cogis
    Pectora? quiduè tuo non est violabile telo?
35   Quin (verum si fama refert, et prisca vetustas)
    Saturnum, Martémque tuis, ipsúmque Tonantem
    Vulnera turbarunt haud irrita facta sagittis,
    Ille licèt senij vicio subfrigidus esset,
    Alter multiplici clypeo munitus, et ære,
40   Tertius horrendo metuendus fulminis ictu.
    Quìn matrem quoque dira tuam transfixit arundo,
    Eius et vberibus, quæ te lactârat, inhæsit.
    Nec tua ponticolis nimiùm vesana pepercit
    Dextera numinibus. Stygiæ neque rector abyssi
45   Spicula maioris potuit sanare tyranni,
    Telis antè tuis cùm pectore saucius esset.
    Dum Cælo, Pontóque noces, Erebóque profundo,
    (Eheu) terrigenæ quid nos speremus amantes?
      O, qui me fluctus, quis me telluris hiatus
50   Pertæsum tetricæ vitæ, deglutiat ore
    Chasmatico, viuúmque nigro dimittat Auerno?
[B2] Cælicolæ (nam vos etiam torquemini amore)
    Si pietas vobis aliqua est, si pauperis alta
    Vulnera pastoris cælestia numina spectant,
55   Eripite hanc animam dubijs quibus vndíque curis

Beating dust with wings, and feathers fowly beeraying,   25
Beating breast with beack til bloud come freshly abounding,
Til lyfe gushing forth with bloud goe ioyntly together,
So did Amyntas mourne, such true loue made him a mourner.
  O what a vyle boy's this, what a greeuous wound, what a
    weapon?
O what a dart is this that sticks so fast to my heart roote,   30
Like as roots to the trunck, or like as vine to the Elmetree,
Iuy ioynd to the walls, or greene mos cleeues to the foule
    ponds.
O pitiles lous-god: poore louers how be we plagued?   [B3ᵛ]
O strong dart of loue which each thing speedily pearceth
This dart God Saturne, God Mars, and great God of al Gods   35
Ioue himself did wound, vnles that fame doe beely them:
Although God Saturne were old and like to a crusht crabb,
Although Mars were armd with try'd, Vulcanian armour,
Although Ioue with fire and thunder maketh a rumbling.
Yea thine owne mother, thine owne inuincible arrow   40
Hurt: and prickt those papps which thou wast wont to be
    sucking.
Neither spar'st thou him that raigns in watery kingdome,
Neither spar'st thou him that rules in feareful Auernus,
Pluto knows what it is with a paltery boy to be troubled,
Neptune knows what it is by a blinde boyes check to be   45
    mated.
Then since heauen, seas, and hell are nought by thee spared,
Earth and earth dwelling louers must looke to be pinched.
  O what gaping earth wil Amintas greedily swallow,
O what goulf of Seas, and deepes, will quickly deuoure him?
And bring him lyuing to the deadmens souls in Auernus.   50
  Gods of skies (for loue hath pearst oft vp to the heauens)
Yf pity moue your harts, if you from stately Olympus
Can vouchsafe to behold these inward wounds of Amintas,
Free this troubled soule from cares and infinite anguish,

27 *omit* D]

31 as roots . . . like as vine B C E] as roots . . . life as vine A; a root
. . . like a vine D

32 *omit* D   46 heauen] heauens D hell] hells D
36 them:] them. A–E   50 deadmens] dead men E

Opprimitur, longis placidam concedite pacem
Litibus: Atque vtinam subijssem fata suprema,
Dum nostro mecum cecinit mea Phyllis in agro,
Donec me gremio tulit, amplexúque fouebat,
60 Donec in vmbrosa sylua requieuimus ambo.
Tunc etenim fœlix potui deponere vitam,
Illáque pallentes orbes morientis amici
Clausisset blandè, quæ viuo sola placebat.
Sed quorsum toties venientem poscere mortem,
65 Atque perire iuuat? me non optante peribo,
Obtinuit tantas animi contractio vires.
Deficiunt solidæ vires, ac pristina virtus
Membrorum, vitǽque calor, ceu fumus, in auras
Effugit, et iuuenem premit immatura senectus.
70 O sors infœlix, quid non coguntur amantes
"Inuita ratione pati? furiosa libido
"Non vllos vnquam fugit imperterrita casus.
Ah chari quoties obliuia nominis opto?
Ah quoties opto pro Phyllide summa tulisse
75 Fata tamen? Vario mens fluctuat anxia motu,
"Vt nutans inter Scyllam sæuámque Charybdin
"Naufragio vicina ratis, quam iustus vtrínque
[B2ᵛ] "Impedit, impellítque timor, dum turbine pontus
"Æstuat, et fragilis ligni, quod inhæret arenis,
80 "Heu, lacerum findit latus, immergítque profundo.
  Sed quìd ego veteres nequicquam lugeo flammas

71 inuita] in uita 85.

[42]

End these endles toyls, bring ease by my death to my deaths-   55
   wound.
   O that I had then dy'd when Phillis liu'd with Amintas,
In fyelds when Phillis sang songs of loue with Amintas,
In fyelds when Phillis kist and embraced Amintas,
In fyelds when Phillis slept vnder a tree with Amintas,
Blest had Amintas beene, if death had taken Amintas,   60
So my Phillis might haue come and sate by my death-bed,
Closing these eye-lidds of dead, but blessed Amyntas,
Blest, that he dy'd in her arms, that his eyes were closd by her
   owne hands.
But what, alas, do I meane, for death thus still to be wishing
Foole that I am? For death coms quickly without any wish-   65
   ing.
Inward griefe of troubled soule hath brought me to deaths
   doore,
Woonted strength doth faile, my lyms are fainty with an-
   guish,
Vitall heate is gone like vnto a smoke, to a vapor,
Yeasterday but a boy, and now grayheaded Amintas.
   O luckles louers, how alwaies are wee beewitched?   70
What contrarieties, what fancyes flatly repugnant,   [B4]
How many deaths, liues, hopes, feares, ioyes, cares stil do
   wee suffer?
O that I could forget Phillis, many times am I wishing,
O that I had dy'd, for Phillis, manie times am I wishing,
Thus distracted I am ten thousand times by my wishing.   75
Like to a shipp through whyrling goulfs vnsteadily passing,
Floating here and there, hence thence, with daunger on each
   side,
Fearing Scyllaes iawes, and mouth of greedy Charibdis:
Whylst by the rage of Sea brusd shipp sticks fast to the
   quick sands,
And by the mighty rebounding waues is lastly deuoured.   80
   But what, alas, doe I meane mine olde loue stil to be
   mourning,

61 come and sate] sitten downe D
63 by] with D   72 deaths, liues] lyues, deaths D
68 to] or D   79 quick sands] quick sand C E

Immemor officij, pecudúmque, et vitis, et agri?
Lædentur pecudes austero flamine venti;
Lactea nec ludet cum nigro vacca iuuenco.
85   Antibus effractis teneram sus improba vitem
Eruet immundo rictu, non sepe virenti
Septam: nec ramos procurua falce putatos
Iam salicis quisquam sinuoso vinciet vdæ
Vimine: nec tumidis parcet mala pica racemis.
90   Et, quodcunque ferunt Borealia frigora damnum,
Inculti nudíque mei patientur agelli.
    Mecum piniferæ suspiria fundite rupes,
Mecum desertæ syluæ spirate querelas,
Mecum conspicui lachrymas emittite fontes,
95   Et viduæ vites, desolatǽque myricæ.
Vos etenim dulcem tenuistis Phyllida rupes,
Vosque quiescentem laudastis Phyllida syluæ,
Et vitrei fontes illi blandire soletis,
Et vos gemmiferæ vites, paruǽque myricæ.
100   Nox erat, et sese pastor sub tecta recêpit.

[B3]   *QVERELA SEXTA.*

Post obitum nymphæ spargebat lumine montes
Sexta dies, humilísque suos ex æquore Titan
Iam Tartessiaco currus, madidósque reduxit
Alipedes, purum spirantes naribus ignem
5   Elatis: cùm molle pecus, tectúmque relinquens,
In steriles campos solus concessit Amyntas,
Fletibus ora sibi fœdans, et pectora pugnis.
Talibus et verbis demens iter omne replebat,
Qualia questus erat quondam Rhodopeius Orpheus
10   Thrëiceas inter rupes, aut fluminis Hæbri

2 humilisque 85] humidosque *would read better.*

[*44*]

Forgetting pastures, and flocks, and vines by my mourning?
My naked pastures with fludds are like to bee drowned,
My fyelds vntilled with thorns are like to be pestred,
My poore sheepe and goats with cold are like to be pinched,   85
My prety black bullock wil come no more to my white cowe,
And by the swynes foule snout my vines are like to be rooted,
For want of walling, for want of customed hedging,
Ranck boughes in vinetree ther's no body now to be cutting,
Cutt boughs with wythy twiggs ther's no body now to bee   90
    binding,
Pecking pyes from grapes ther's no body now to bee keeping.
You rocks helpe me to mourn: rocks, pynetrees loftily bear-
    ing:
You woods helpe me to mourne: woods alwayes wont to be
    silent:
You wells helpe me to mourne: wells cleare and like to the
    Christal:
Vines forlorne, forsaken shrubbs lament with Amintas: 95
On you rocks many times Phillis was woont to be walking,
In you woods many times Phillis was wont to be sitting,
With you wells many times Phillis was wont to be smyling,
And you vines and shrubbs Phillis was wont to be fingring.
    Now 'twas iust darknight, and home came seelly Amintas.   100

THE SIXT LAMENTATION.   [B4ᵛ]

SInce Phillis buriall, six times sprang light fro the moun-
    taines,
Six times had Titan brought backe his coach fro the mainsea,
And flying horses, with salt waues all to bedashed,
With puft vp nosthrils great fire flames lustilie breathing:
When to the wild woods went careles, yet careful Amintas,   5
Leauing flock in fold, no creatures companie keeping
Beating breast with fist, with teares face foulie defacing,
Filling waies as he went, with such and so manie wailings
As were sometimes made by the sweet Rhodopeïan Orpheus,
When by the rocks of Thrace, by the fatall water of Hæbrus,   10

96 was *faults escaped*] way A

Iuxta fatales ripas in cespite viuo,
Cùm bis ereptam scelerati legibus Orci
Eurydicen lugeret amans, et pectine blando,
(Voce sed intensos ad neruos antè parata)
15 Lamentísque feras, volucres, truncósque moueret.
Hæc pastoris erat vox ærumnosa dolentis.
   Hei mihi, quòd lucem cupiant animalia quæque,
Paruuláque Auroræ cantu gratetur Acanthis,
Dum rubet in prima surgentis parte diei.
20 Hei mihi, quòd tenebras cupiant animalia quæque,
Et gratus saturis eluceat Hesperus hœdis,
Dum rubet in gelidæ prima caligine noctis.
Nec tenebræ misero, neque lux arridet Amyntæ:
Fallo diem gemitu, gemitu quoque tempora noctis
25 Fallo; nec vlla dies, neque nox caret vlla querelis.
[B3ᵛ]   Sin quis miretur, tam longùm tristis Amyntas
Viuere quî possim, tam sæuo saucius igne,
Et vitæ putet esse breuis, neque posse manere
Quod caret alterna requie: miracula nescit,
30 Quæ facit immortalis Amor. Non finibus vllis
"Illum communis naturæ regula claudit,
"Alma nec astringit Ratio, non altus Olympus
"Legibus ætherijs illum, non Iuppiter ipse
Continet imperio, qui nutu nubila cogit.
35 Illius impulsu priuigno Phædra pudico
Mentitis læthum inuexit crudele tabellis.
Illius hortatu fratrem temeraria Colchis
In frusta abscissum vento commisit inani.
Illius inuento thalami pertæsa virilis
40 Impia Pasiphaë tauro se miscuit albo.
Illius admonitu perijt Chironis alumnus
Troiugenæ blanda deceptus fraude puellæ.

His sweet Euridice with most sweet voice he bewailed,
Euridice twice lost, by the cursed lawes of Auernus,
When sweet voice sweet harpe ioined most sweetlie together,
Made both birds and beasts and stocks and stones to be
    mourning.
  Euerie beast in field wisheth day light to be comming,   15
Morning starre by the birds in fields is sweetlie saluted,
As soone as she begins by the breake of daie to be peeping.
Euerie beast in field wisheth darke night to be comming,
Euning starre to the kids well fed coms hartelie welcom,
As soone as she begins by the nights aproch to be shining.   20
Neither daie nor night can please displeased Amintas;
All daie long doe I mourne, and all night long am I mourning,
No dai's free fro my plaints, and no night's free fro my plain-
    ing.
  Who so thinks it straunge, that thus tormented Amintas,
Can thus long endure: who thinks it straunge, that Amintas,   25
Lius, yet takes no rest, but still lius, still to be dying;
This man knows not, alas, that loue is dailie triumphant,
This man knowes not, alas, that loue can worke manie won-
    ders,
Loue can abide no law, loue alwaies lous to be lawles,
Loue altreth nature, rules reason, maistreth Olimpus   30
Lawes, edicts, decrees; contemns Ioue mightilie thundring,
Ioue that rules and raigns, that with beck bendeth Olimpus.
Loue caus'de Hippolitus with bry'rs and thorns to be man-   [C1]
    gled,
For that he had foule loue of lusting Phædra refused.
Loue made Absyrtus with sisters hands to be murdred,   35
And in peeces torne, and here and there to be scattred.
Loue forc'd Pasiphae mans companie long to be loathing,
And for a white buls flesh, buls companie long to be lusting.
Loue and luring lookes of louelie Polixena caused
Greekish Achilles death, when he came to the Church to be   40
    wedded.

12 Auernus] Auermus A	22 mourning] playnyng D
14 stocks] flocks E	23 plaining] mourning D
15 day light B C D E] darke night A	28 omit D

Eius et immiti percussus arundine binis
Parebat dominis, scuticámque pauebat herilem,
45 Anteà, totum humeris qui cælum sustentasset.
Illéque Læandrum cumulo submersit aquarum
Nuda procelloso tendentem brachia ponto.
Eius et insidijs aquilæ, pastoris, Echidnæ,
Flammarum, cygni, pluuiæ, tauri, Amphytrionis,
50 Dictynnæ, et Satyri latuit sub imagine falsa,
Qui rotat immensi sinuosa volumina mundi.
[B4]   Cur autèm cæci pueri crudelia gesta
Consiliúmque nocens memoro, cædésque nefandas,
Cuius fine caret nimis importuna tyrannis?
55 Non misero quisquam magis est expertus Amynta
Quantas ille habeat vires, qualésque sagittas.
Hei mihi, quàm sequitur lenti vestigia calcis,
Quò me cunque feram? facit et crudescere pectus
Mille modis, nostro dum singula quæque dolori
60 Respondent, ego seu nigrantes abiete lucos,
Seu iuga celsa petam, riui seu rauca fluenta
Labilis, aut ripæ viridantes desuper herbas
Incumbam, salicis gelida flauentis in vmbra?
    Dum queror in syluis, tacitò lugubria syluæ
65 Increpitant mecum, nutántque cacumina summa
Intonsæ quercus, atque aëriæ cupressus.
Dumque fleo, leuibus ventis agitata susurros
Ac sibilos ædit syluarum gloria pinus,
Ac si magnus ei meus innotescat amaror.
70 Nec citiùs digno Phyllis cumulatur honore
Luctibus in nostris, quàm pando gutture deflet
Daulias ales Itym: comes, ô, dulcissima flenti.
"Et viduus turtur veteri gemebundus ab orno

Loue made Alcides that great inuincible Heros,
Maister of all monsters, at length to be whipt by a mistres.
Loue drowned Læander swimming to the beawtiful Hero,
Vnto the towne Cestos, from towne of cursed Abydos.
Loue made Ioue, that's ruler of earth, and ruler of heauen,   45
Like to a seely shepheard and like to the fruitful Echidna,
Like to a fire, to a swan, to a showre, to a bull, to an Ægle,
Sometimes Amphytrion, sometimes Dyctinna resembling.
    But what neede I to shew this blindboyes surly behauiour,
Lewd pranks, false policies, slye shifts, and wily deuises,   50
Murdring minde, hardhart, dead hand, bent bow, readie ar-
    rowes?
No body knows better what bitter griefe is abounding
In loues lewd kingdome, then luckles louer Amintas.
Whether I go to the groues, or whether I climbe to the moun-
    tains,
Whether I walk by the banks, or whether I looke to the   55
    fountains,
Loue stil waits at an inch, and neuer leaus to be pinching.
Euerie thing complains, and aunswereth vnto my playning,
Euerie thing giues cause and new increase to my mourning.
    If that I mourne in woods, these woods seeme al to be
        mourning,
And broadbrauncht Oake trees their vpright tops to be bow-   60
    ing.
If that I sigh or sobb, this pine tree straight by the shaking,
This peereles pine tree for company seems to bee pyning,
As though himselfe felt th'enduring pangs of Amintas.
    And that byrd of Thrace, my woful companie keeping,
Cries, and cals for Itys, with monstrous villany murdred,   65
Murdred, alas, by the diu'lish crafts and means of a mother,
Boyled, alas, by the merciles hart and hand of a sister,
Eaten, alas, by the cursed mouth and teeth of a father.
And poore Turtle-doue her mates good company missing,

58 Euerie] Euere A; Euery B C D E new] fresh D
66 diu'lish crafts and means] merciles hart and hand B C E, ... hands D
67 omit B C D E

"Sæpiùs, heu, nostros imitatur murmure questus.
75   Dumque ego cliuosi ac sterilis fastigia montis
Conscendo, fragilem passum syluestris oliuæ
Sustentans baculo, violentáque sydera diris
[B4ᵛ] Impeto, florentem quoniam violâre iuuentam
Phyllidis, heu, nomen mihi Phyllidis illicò voce
80   Quintuplici repetit vastis e rupibus Eccho.
Cum gemitu gemitus, et murmure murmura nectens.
Tum fera si qua meas audit vicina querelas,
Accedit, blandèque meo sub poplite cumbens
Fert caudam crispantem vtero, dorsùmque bacillo
85   Palpari patitur, nostri miserata doloris:
"Qualis Romuleo seruata leæna Theatro,
"Androdo mortem quæ condonabat amico.
O, si tanta foret pietas fatalibus astris,
Phyllide non viduârer ego, neque Phyllis Amynta.
90   Dumque ego propter aquas fixus sub margine ripæ
Intueor lachrymis, gemitúque tumescere fluctus,
Fœda mihi querulæ faciunt conuitia ranæ.
Tum fortassis Hylam dubiosa mente reuoluens,
Naiades, heu, supplex oro, genubúsque reflexis,
95   Vt me sicut Hylam vitreas traxisse sub vndas
Dignentur, condántque diem vitámque perosum.
Sed frustrata ferunt venti mea vota proterui,
Sic nihil ex animo tristi succedit Amyntæ,
Quem grauium infœlix circundat Lerna malorum.
100   Nunc humiles ædes sub nocte reuisit Amyntas.

Sitts on a naked bough, and keeps mee company mourning.   70
When that I climbe to the ragged rocks, and creepe to the [C1ᵛ]
   mountains,
Staying feeble knees with a staffe, for feare of a falling,
If that I then curse death, and raile on desteny fatal,
For marring that face, those cheeks, those yuory fingers
Of my sweete Phillis: Phillis coms back with an eccho,   75
Eccho returns Phillis fiue times fro the rocks, fro the moun-
   tains.
Euery beast which heares these woful plaints of Amintas,
Coms, and sitts him downe twixt leggs of woful Amintas:
Suffers back to be stroakt with staffe of mourneful Amintas:
Claps his tayle t'is belly beelowe, and moans with Amintas: 80
As that good lionesse, which first was cur'd by a Romaine,
In Romain theater gaue life for life to the Romaine.
O if such pity were in desteny no pitie taking,
Phillis I should not misse, nor Phillis misse of Amintas.
If that I come to the banks and cast mine eyes to the waters,   85
Waters augmented with these my watery fountains,
Then these foulemouth'd froggs with iarring tunes do molest
   me,
So that I am compeld with bowing knees to be praying,
Praying vnto the nimphs in bowrs of water abyding,
That they would vouchsafe to receiue my carkas among   90
   them,
And fro the sight of man, fro the light of sunne to remoue it,
As that loued Hylas they sometimes friendly receaued.
But yet I wish in vaine, and nought can I get by my wishing,
And of my wishing these lewd winds make but a whistling.
So nothing contents poore mal-contented Amintas,   95
Clogd with an heape of cares, and clos'd in an hell ful of
   horror.
   Then to his homely Cabin, by the moone light hasted
   Amintas.

70 *omit* D	80 moans] moan's AB; moanes CE;
71 that] *omit* E	*omit* D
78 woful *faults escaped*] wofull A	88 praying, B C D E] praying. A
79 suffers] suffring D	96 an hell] a hell D

[B5] *QVERELA SEPTIMA*.

Septima lux noctem pepulit, cùm tristis Amyntas
Immites macro pascens sub pectore flammas,
Paupere de tecto syluis successit opacis,
Inque pias lachrymas rorantia lumina soluens
5   Surdis questus erat nequicquam talia ventis.
    Non sum, qualis eram, lasciui gloria ruris,
Non agilis fœnum dentato cogere rastro
In teretes cumulos, non flagro grana saligno
Tundere, non vites sinuosa falce putare,
10   Non stiuam retinere manu, et proscindere terram,
Non scabros curare greges, non tempore festo
Alternis pedibus campum pulsare sonantem,
Nec calamos inflare leues, neque dicere versus.
Heu, solitum perijt robur, mihi mensque sepulta est,
15   Postquam perpetuo clauduntur lumina somno
Phyllidis, æterno quæ lumine digna fuerunt.
Deliciæ nostræ Phylli, dum viua manebas,
Dulces deliciæ: quæ dudum rustica virgo
Ingenio tecum potuit conferre, vel arte,
20   Eloquio dulci, gestu, vultuué sereno?
Tantùm, Phylli, tibi reliquæ cessere puellæ,
"Quantùm vpupæ cygnis, quantùm saliunca rosetis,
"Quantùm oleis salices, philomelæ cedit hyrundo.
Nec minùs ornabat tua tum præsentia turbas
25   "Fœmineas, decorat vitem quam pensilis vua,
[B5ᵛ] Laurea quàmque hortum, seges aruum, armentáque taurus.
Ipsa tuæ, quæ dum superest, vox inclyta laudis
Omnia sic superat nostri præconia ruris,
Torqueat vt pulchræ auersas Amarillydis aures
30   Omnibus vna magis dum vult formosa videri.
Illa sed in lachrymas liuentes soluat ocellos

THE SEVENTH LAMENTATION. [C2]

SIxe nights now were past, and seu'nth day hastened on-
     ward,
When with fretting cares, al spent and wasted Amintas,
Went to the wood, stark wood, with great extremitie weeping,
And to the dul deafe winds his late loss freshly bewayling.
O how much this Amintas is altred from that Amintas,   5
Which was wont to be capten of euery company rurall?
Nothing nimble I am with willowe staffe to be threshing,
Nor with toothed rake round heycocks for to be making.
Nothing nimble I am, my braunched vines to be cutting,
Nor with sharpe edg'd sucke my fruitful soile to be plowing. 10
Nothing nimble I am my scabbed sheepe to be curing,
Nor with leaping lads, with tripping trulls to be daunsing.
Nothing nimble I am sweete rimes and songs to be making,
Nor sweete songs and rymes on pleasant pype to be playing.
My sense is dulled, my strength extreamely decayed,   15
Since that faire Phillis my loue did leaue me for euer,
Who was worthy to liue, and worthy to loue me for euer.
   Phillis, faire Phillis, thou dearling deare of Amintas,
What lasse durst compare with dearling deare of Amintas,
For witt, for learning, for face, for seemely behauiour?   20
My sweete lasse Phillis was no more like to the gray gowns,
And countrey milkemaids, then nightingale to the lapwing,
Rose to the greene willow, or siluer swan to the swallow.
Phillis amidst faire maids did fairemaids company count-
     nance,
As ripe corne doth fields, as clustred grapes do the vinetrees, 25
As stout bulls do the droues, as bayleaus beautifie gardens.
   Phillis name and fame, which is yet freshly remembred,
Passed abroad so farre, so farre surpast Amarillis,
As that it yrkt and grieu'd disdainful prowd Amaryllis,
Who stil thought her selfe for beauties praise to be peereles. 30
But let her hart ful of hate stil pine, let her eyes ful of enuy

1 onward *faults escaped*] outward A   8 heycocks *faults escaped*] heycock A
4 loss] lost A   25 vinetrees, B C D E] vinetrees. (?) A
6 capten *faults escaped*] captein A   30 for] far E   54 morning,] eu'ning? D

[*53*]

Æmula virgo tui, dabitur tibi pristina palma.
"Non etenim dignæ occumbunt cum corpore laudes,
"Vera nec in summo sordescit funere virtus.
35 Ista sed extinctæ præconia dicere quid nunc
Attinet, et cæcos fando renouare dolores?
"Est melius nunquam fœlicia tempora nosse,
"Quàm, post blanditias Fortunæ, fata maligna,
"Nec reparanda pati infortunia sortis iniquæ.
40 Quid mihi iam prodest, olim sub sole corusco
Molliter exceptum tepido gremióque sinúque
Languentes carpsisse mea cum Phyllide somnos,
Vt clam cum Mopso nobis foret inuidus Æglon?
Quid tandem prodest, per luxuriantia prata
45 Demetijsse vnà fragrantes pollice flores,
Intyba, narcissos, et purpureos hyacinthos,
Liliáque, et violas, casiámque, rosásque, thymúmque,
Et textis Satyros, Charitésque ornasse coronis?
Quid iuuat, in duris hærentia mora rubetis,
50 Et fraga, et teretes baccas, et mitia corna
Collexisse simul, calathósque implesse colurnos?
[B6] "Quìd totiès cupidis auidè luctantia labris
Oscula iunxisse, et molles traxisse loquelas
In multam noctem? fragili quìd nomina buxo in-
55 sculpsisse, et solo votum violabile fato?
Heu, perij, postquam Phyllis, charissima Phyllis
(Heu) perijt: quìd enim faciam sine Phyllide viuus?
Non autem perij morbo correptus, vt illa,
Sit nisi morbus amor: sed lentis ignibus vstus
60 Paulatìm morior, Mora morte ferocior ipsa est.

Stil be resolu'd in teares, Phillis surmounts Amaryllis.
Phillis dead is aliue, and so shal liue to the worlds end,
Phillis praise shal scape from death and graue to the worlds [C2ᵛ]
 end.
But what auails it alas dead Phillis now to be praysing?   35
Phillis, alas, is dead, tis too late now to be praysing,
And to renew old thoughts and fond conceipts by my praising.
Better it is to be low and neuer climbe to a kingdome,
Then fro the scepter againe to be tumbled downe to the
 dunghil.
For what auails it now that Phillis lulled Amintas,   40
Lull'd him a sleepe in her arms and slept her selfe with Amin-
 tas,
Vnder a cooling shade from scorching beams to defend vs,
Which sight made Æglon and Mopsus teeth to be watrie?
Or what auails it now t'haue gathered iointly together
Fragrant hearbs and flowres by the mantled fields, by the 45
 meddows,
Daffadil, and Endiue, with mourning flowre Hyacinthus,
Thyme, Casia, Violets, Lillies, and sweete prety roses
For nymphs and woodgods gay garlands duely preparing?
Or what auails it now t'haue pluckt at strawbery brambles,
Blackebery briers t'haue spoild, t'haue bared mulbery 50
 braunches,
With such countrie fruits our baskets heauily loading?
 Or what auails it now t'haue giu'n her so many kisses,
And t'haue taken againe in like sort so many kisses?
 Or what auails it now t'haue drawn our talk to the morn-
 ing,
Or t'haue made our names with box tree barke to be growing, 55
Names and vowes which nought but death could cause to
 be broken?
Wofull wretch that I am, Phillis forsaks me for all this,
And forsaken of her, death hath possest me for all this.
And yet I am not sick (vnles that loue be a sicknes)
But death coms creeping, and lingring life is a flytting, 60
And this differring of death is worse then a dying.

55 names] name E   58 her, death B C D E] her death, A

Talis enim morior, qualis qui viscera cæcis
Æstubus affligi sceleratæ crimine matris
Sensijt, ac absens inuitis ignibus arsit.
Non caret vlla dies lachrymis, non hora laboris
65 Expers vlla sui: me, me fœlicior ille est,
Qui viuum rutilis ignem furatus ab astris,
Et Superûm iussu Scythica sub rupe ligatus
Pulpantem volucrem fœcundo pectore pascit.
O bone Pan, Fauníque puellis turba benigna,
70 Huc celerem conferte gradum, positísque cicutis
Multiforis, cantúque leui, placidísque choræis,
Vestras iam lachrymas lachrymis adiungite nostris,
Et mecum fletu miserando aspergite bustum
Phyllidis: illa etenim vobis dedit annua liba,
75 Et placuit vobis, inter lasciua papillas
Dum lusit niueas, formosior omnibus vna,
Et reliquas nymphas gestu decorabat honesto,
[B6ᵛ] "Oréque sydereo, croceis hedera alba corymbis
"Vt laurum decorat, formosis brachia nectens
80 "Brachiolis: nitidúmque vt perlucentibus aurum
"Chrysolitus radijs ornat, nitidissimus ipse.
Secum delicias, et maxima gaudia ruris
Abstulit, ac miseris iacet (heu) ploranda colonis.
Hortéque iam luge, ô, exculte, ardentibus illa
85 Solibus arentem gelidis quem vespere primo
Sæpè rigabat aquis, et blando calce premebat.
Vosque, ô, perspicui fontes, quos illa beato
Afflauit vultu, viridi lanugine tectis

Lingring fire by degrees hath spent and wasted Amintas,
As Meleager of old, whose life was left in a firebrand,
Firebrand cast to the fire by the murdring hands of a mother,
When fatall firebrand burning did burne Meleager.   65
Euery day do I weepe, and euery houre am I wayling,
Euery houre and day dismal to the wretched Amintas,
Yea much more wretched, then that poore seely Prometheus,
Who for his aspyring, for stealing fire from Olympus,
Was by the Gods decrees fast bound with chains to the   70
    mountaine
Caucasus, huge and cold, where hee's compelled an Eagle,
Eagle stil feeding, with his owne heart still to be feeding.   [C3]
    O Pan, ô Fauni, that loue with maids to bee liuely,
Leaue your pipes, your songs, your daunce, leaue off to be
    liuely,
Ioyne your teares with Amintas teares, and mourne with   75
    Amintas,
And mourne for Phillis, for Phillis leaueth Amintas.
Phillis for your sake fine wafers duely prepared,
Phillis pleasd your eyes whilst Phillis daintily daunced,
Phillis amidst faire maids was deemed stil to be fayrest,
And gaue grace to the rest with her eyes and comely be-   80
    hauiour,
As faire Laurel trees be adornd with beautiful iuye,
As fine golde is adornd by the shining light of a iasper.
Since death of Phillis no ioyes enioyeth Amintas,
Euery good thing's gone: Phillis tooke euery good thing,
Countrey soile laments and countrey men be a weeping.   85
    And thou garden greene now powre forth plaints with
        Amintas,
Phillis thy sweet banks and bedds did water at eu'ning,
Phillis amidst thy flowres alwayes wast wont to be walking,
But now no walking, but now no water at euning,
Now best flowre is dead, now Phillis gone fro the garden.   90
And you Christall springs with streames of siluer abounding,
Where faire Phillis saw faire Phillis face to be shyning,

88 wast] was B C D E

E specubus largum lachrymarum mittite flumen.
90 Nam non tangetis fœlices amplius ora
Phyllidis, ora Iouis coniungi digna labellis.
   Vosque ô, frondosæ valles, syluǽque silentes,
In quibus est niueas depascere sueta capellas
Inter custodes pecudum, rigidósque bubulcos,
95 Ereptam propero fato lugete puellam.
   Sed Pan, Fauni, horte, et fontes, valles, syluǽque
Comprimite, ô, luctus, et me permittite solum
Soluier in lachrymas ad lamentabile bustum:
In mortem addetur mea mors, in funera funus.
100   Hæc fatus tuguri repetit sub vespere culmen.

[B7]   *QVERELA OCTAVA.*

Post mortem teneræ, tumulatáque virginis ossa,
Cum pulsis tenebris iam lux octaua colores
Restituit rebus, densas miserandus Amyntas
Ingreditur syluas iterum per opaca viarum.
5 Atque illic tandem subter myrto impendente
Procumbit lassus: nec virginis immemor, altum
Sic fatur, longis singultibus ilia pulsans.
   Ergonè surripuit totius gaudia ruris
Vna puella? ouium custodibus vna puella
10 Tantos imposuit luctus, lamentáque tanta?

Powre forth fludds of teares from those your watery foun-
    tains,
From those your fountains with greene mos all to be smeared:
Phillis wil no more see Phillis sitt by the fountains,   95
Phillis wil no more her lipps apply to the fountains,
Lippes to be ioyn'd to the lipps of Ioue that ruleth Olympus.
  And you darkesome dales, and woods aye wont to be silent,
Where she amidst the shepheards, and toiling boysterus
    heard men,
Her milkwhite shee goats many times was wont to be feeding, 100
Lament and mourne for this nymphs vntimely departure.
  But Pan, and Fauni, but garden greene of Amintas,
But you springs, and dales, and woods aye wont to be silent,
Leaue of your mourning, Ile giue you leaue to be silent,
Leaue to be silent stil, giue you me leaue to bee mourning, 105
Leaue to be mourning stil, let this most heauie departure,
This death of Phillis bring wished death to Amintas.
  Here did he pause for a while, and home at night he re-
    turned.

THE EIGHT LAMENTATION.   [C3ᵛ]

SInce death of Phillis, since Phillis burnt by Amyntas,
Since Phillis burnt bones were chested duly, the eighth time,
Night gaue place to the light, and euning vnto the morning:
When to the woods so wilde, to the wilde beasts dangerus
    harbors,
Forsaking hye wayes, by the bye wayes passed Amintas: 5
And there sets him downe al wearied vnder a myrtle,
For griefe stil groning, with deepe sighs heauily panting,
Stil Phillis naming, stil Phillis feintily calling.
And must one wench thus take all the delights fro the
    countrey?
And must one wench thus make euery man to be mourning? 10
Euery man whose flocks on these hills vse to be feeding?

99 boysterus *faults escaped*] boisterous A   heard men] Heardsmen D
1 *omit* D
2 Since Phillis burnt bones] Now since fayre Phillis was D eighth] eight C E
9 delights] delyte D

Et spargit lachrymas Æglon, tunicáque Menalcas
Induitur nigra, quià mortem Phyllis obiuit?
Et gemitus ædit Corydon, cantúmque querelis
Tityrus immiscet, quià mortem Phyllis obiuit?
15 Et paulùm posuit veteres Amaryllis amores,
Damœtásque suos, quià mortem Phyllis obiuit?
Et subitò pingui macer est mihi taurus in aruo,
Et pecus omne dolet, quià mortem Phyllis obiuit?
Et lachrymæ fiunt fontes, suspiria venti,
20 Cunctáque mutantur, quià mortem Phyllis obiuit?
Nunc igitur quid ego, cui charior omnibus illa
Semper erat mihi quique oculis dilectior hisce
Semper erat, quid agam iam desolatus Amyntas?
Eheu, cur vitam moror exhaurire dolendo?
25 Candida (me miserum) Phyllis caprimulga, capellas
[B7ᵛ] Qua pascente, domum referebant vbera tenta,
Dulcius effluxit compressis lacque papillis:
Qua præsens ætas miscere coagula nullam
Nouit, et agricolis componere liba priorem,
30 Aut fragilem viridi fiscellam texere hibisco,
Aut per prata choros pago ductare stupente:
Qua coryli cupiere capi, dum sedit in agris,
Et prono in gremium nutabat vertice laurus:
Hæc (inquam) Phyllis, Phyllis, defuncta, sepulta est.
35 Ah quotiès illa mecum miscente loquelas
Collexi Dryadis pulchras pictásque corollas?
Ah quoties mecum scabro cantauit in antro,
Syluestrésque meæ versus coniunxit auenæ?
Ah quotiès vinxit me mollibus illa lacertis,

The eighth Lamentation

And must Æglon weepe, and must that friendly Menalcas
Weare his mourning roab, for death of my bony Phillis?
And must good Coridon lament, must Tityrus alter
His pleasant melodies, for death of my bony Phillis?   15
And must Damœtas for griefe leaue of to be louing?
Must Amarillis leaue, for death of my bony Phillis?
And must drooping bull consume as he goes by the meddowe?
Must sheepe looke lowring, for death of my bony Phillis?
And must sighs seeme windes? must teares seeme watery   20
    fountains?
And must each thing change for death of my bony Phillis?
O then what shal I do, for death of my bony Phillis?
Since that I lou'd bonylasse Phillis more dearely then al
    these.
Since that I lou'd her more then I loue these eyes of Amyntas.
O then what shal I do forlorne forsaken Amintas,   25
What shal I doe, but die, for death of my bony Phillis?
Phillis who was wont my flocke with care to bee feeding,
Phillis who was wont my mylch shee goats to be milking,
Phillis who was wont, (most handsome wench of a thousand)
Either clouted creame, or cakes, or curds to be making,   30
Either fine basketts of bulrush for to be framing,
Or by the greene meddows gay dauncing dames to be leading,
Phillis whose bosome filbeards did loue to be filling,   [C4]
Phillis for whose sake greene laurel lou'd to be bowing,
Phillis, alas, sweete lasse Phillis, this braue bony Phillis,   35
Is dead, is buried, maks all good company parted.
O how oft Phillis conferd in fields with Amintas?
Whilst for nymphs of woods gay garlands framed Amintas.
O how oft Phillis did sing in caues with Amintas,
Ioyning her sweete voice to the oaten pipe of Amintas?   40
O how oft Phillis clypt and embraced Amintas,

23 Since] Syth D

24 Since] Syth D

After 26 D *adds line* Phillis whoe was woont with bowe and shafts to be
shooting

38 *omit* D

40   Ah quotiès, miseræque dedit solamina flammæ
Basia mille, meus quæ vix pateretur ocellus
Inuidus: et morsu petijt, gemuítque remorsa?
Phylli diù (res si qua diù mortalibus vlla est)
Viximus vnanimes, qualis cum turture turtur:
45   Vna fides, amor vnus erat, mens vna duobus.
Cùm fugeres ergò, fuit ah, fuit vtile tecum
Ire mihi, vitæque simul discedere curis.
    Proh dolor, ille decor sub flore emarcuit ipso,
Quo nec amabilius, quo nec formosius vlla
50   Sæcula viderunt quicquam, venturáque quo nil
Ætas aspiciet melius, vel laudibus æquum.
[B8] Sicciné purpureo violæ spoliantur amictu?
Sicciné condensas amittit tempore paruo
Populus alta comas? heu non mutabile fatum.
55   O quotiès tremulis, quandò moribunda iacebat,
Impleui thalamos, tristésque vlulatibus ædes,
Atque vtinam, dixi, febrem de corpore Phœbus
Arceat, aut Phœbo nympháque Coronide natus
Archiatros, tumidam pepulit qui vulneris iram,
60   Hirsuto Cytheræa rubo cum fossa doleret?
Aut vtinam clarus medica Podalyrius arte,
Herbarumué potens morienti Colchis adesset,
Quæ succo potuit lapsam renouare iuuentam?
Aut satus Iapeto sapiens animare figuras
65   Feruore ætherio, gypsóque infundere vitam.
    Talia questus eram, sed multa diuque querenti
Nemo ferebat opem, donec (proh fata nefanda)

How many thousand times hath Phillis kissed Amintas,
Bitten Amintas lipps, and bitten againe of Amintas?
So that Amintas his eyes inuied these lipps of Amintas.
O sweete soule Phillis w'haue liu'd and lou'd for a great while,   45
(If that a man may keepe any mortal ioy for a great while)
Like louing Turtles and Turtledoues for a great while:
One loue, one liking, one sence, one soule for a great while,
Therfore one deaths wound, one graue, one funeral only
Should haue ioyned in one both loue and louer Amintas.   50
   O good God what a griefe is this that death to remember?
For such grace, gesture, face, feature, beautie, behauiour,
Neuer afore was seene, is neuer againe to be lookt for.
O frowning fortune, ô death and desteny dismal:
Thus be the poplar trees that spred their tops to the heauens,   55
Of their flouring leaues despoil'd in an houre, in a moment:
Thus be the sweete violets that gaue such grace to the garden,
Of their purpled roabe despoyld in an houre, in a moment.
   O how oft did I roare and crie with an horrible howling,
When for want of breath Phillis lay feintily gasping?   60
O how oft did I wish that Phœbus would fro my Phillis
Driue this feuer away: or send his sonne from Olympus,
Who, when lady Venus by a chaunce was prickt with a
    bramble,
Healed her hand with his oyles, and fine knacks kept for a
    purpose.
Or that I could perceiue Podalyrius order in healing,   65
Or that I could obtaine Medæas exquisite ointments,
And baths most precious, which old men freshly renewed.
Or that I were as wise, as was that craftie Prometheus,
Who made pictures liue with fire that he stole from Olympus.
Thus did I cal and crie, but no body came to Amintas,   70
Then did I raile and raue, but nought did I get by my railing, [C4ᵛ]
Whilst that I cald and cry'd, and rag'd, and rau'd as a mad
    man,

45 for] *omit* C E
49 Therfore] Thefore A
58 roabe] roabes B C D E
59 roare and crie] cry, and roare D

62 this] that D
64 his] *omit* E purpose.] purpose:
C E; purpose? D
70 Amintas,] Amintas. C E;
Amintas: D

Ante diem rapida consumptam febre puellam
Abstulit atra dies, et funere mersit acerbo.
70   O infausta dies, nigro signanda lapillo,
In qua nulla dedit misero solatia ruri
Cynthius, atra procul caput inter nubila condens;
In qua non dulces cantus auis vlla sonabat,
Et coluber sese pauidus non extulit antro;
75   In qua culminibus dirum fera noctua carmen
Ingemuit, stridore mali prænuncia fati.
O mihi prima dies mortis, vitǽque suprema,
[B8ᵛ] Et quam nulla meo delebunt sæcula corde,
Anteà quam sicco viuant in littore pisces,
80   Quàm teneat ceruos æther, quàm sidera tellus.
Ex quo Phyllis enim morti concessit, Amyntæ
Confusam eripuit mentem, perque ora volutæ
In riuos lachrymæ coëunt, ac æstuat ingens
Imo in corde dolor, mistóque insania luctu,
85   Et furijs agitatus amor, segnísque libido.
     Iupiter humanos semper miserate labores,
Plurima quem pueri fixerunt spicula Diui,
Tuque Pater lucis, qui quondàm pulsus Olympo
Fleuisti pastor Messenia per dumæta,
90   Pastoris miserere mei: miserescite, quæso,
Pauperis, et iuuenis. Tuque, ô, bona noctis alumna,
Quæ vitas adimis, da (non indebita posco
Regna meis curis) Orco considere tandem,
Phyllide cumque mea Stygia sub nocte vagari,

76 prænuncia] prœnumcia 85.

Phillis, alas, Phillis by the burning fitts of a feuer,
Quickly before her day, her daies vnluckily ended.
O dismal deaths day, with black stone still to be noted,   75
Wherein no sunne shin'd, no comfort came fro the heauens,
Wherein clustred clouds had cou'red lightsome Olympus,
Wherein no sweete bird could finde any ioy to be chirping,
Wherein loathsome snakes from dens were loath to be creep-
    ing,
Wherein foule skriche owles did make a detestable howling,   80
And from chimney top gaue woful signes of a mischiefe.
O first day of death, last day of life to Amintas,
Which no day shal driue from soule and hart of Amintas,
Til Neptune dry'de vp withdrawe his fludds fro the fishes,
And skaled fishes liue naked along by the sea shore,   85
Till starrs fal to the ground, til light harts leap to Olympus.
For since Phillis went and left forsaken Amintas,
Ioyes and pleasures went and left forsaken Amintas.
Perplexed speaking, and vaine thoughts only remayned,
Immoderate mourning, and mad loue onely remayned.   90
Thou Ioue omnipotent, which doest with mercie remember
Mortall mens miseries: which knowst what it is to be louing,
And thou god Phœbus that sometimes driu'n from Olympus
Feeding sheepe didst loue, helpe luckles louer Amyntas
Feeding sheepe and goats, help poore man, yong man Amin-   95
    tas.
Thou that abridgest breath, thou daughter deare to the
    darknes,
Cutt this thread of life, dispatch and bring mee to darknes,
Infernal darknes, fit place for mournful Amintas.
So shal Amintas walke and talke in darksome Auernus,

73 Phillis, alas,] Phillis, , alas, A	86 *omit* D harts] hart C E
74 her daies] the daies C	88 *omit* E
78 ioy] way C E	90 *omit* E
79 Wherein] wherein A	95 sheepe and goats] his poore sheepe, D
80 Wherein] wherein A a detest- able B C D E] detestable A	96 breath] death C E thou daughter deare to the] and mak'st our light to be D
81 signes *faults escaped*] signe A	
83 Which] which A	98 mournful] mourner D

[65]

95 Et cupidos miscere sonos, tacitúmque per agrum
Elysij dulces fando recipiscere flammas.
    Heu multas effundo preces, et vota, sed auræ
Omnia discerpunt, et nubibus irrita fundo.
Pulchram igitur quìd non propero per vulnera mortem?
100   Iam Sol Oceanum, tectúmque subibat Amyntas.

[C1]   *QVERELA NONA.*

Iamque vbi nona suos Aurora ostenderet ortus,
Et Phœbus cursu radijsque retexeret orbem,
Pastor fœcundo lachrymis infirma leuabat
Membra thoro, vt sese mox extra tecta referret
5 In tristes latebras, et inhospita regna ferarum,
Quà non inueniat, nisi certa pericula, quicquam.
Dùm verò fessos humeros velabat amictu,
Sæpè graues gemitus imo de pectore ducens,
Phyllidáque ingeminans, iterúmque iterúmque vocauit.
10 Protinus vt lanis artus induxerat, atros
Ingreditur lucos, lucémque domúmque perosus.
Illic (heu) miserè vano correptus amore
Vulnus alit venis, nemorúmque per auia luget:
"Occulta qualis traiectus arundine ceruus,
15 "Intestina dolens fixum per viscera telum,
"Se tacitus abdit syluis, et fata gemendo
"Accelerat, sudore vias et sanguine miscens,
"Nec non lachrymulis multum miserandus obortis
"Dyctamnum frustrà sterili scrutatur in agro.
20 At verò tandem ærumnosa silentia rupit,

So shal Amintas loue with Phillis againe be renued,   100
In fields Elysian Phillis shal liue with Amintas.
Thus do I wish and pray, this praying is but a pratling,
And these wishing words but a blast, but a winde, but a
    whistling.
Dye then Amyntas Dye, for dead is thy bony Phillis.
   Phœbus went to the sea: to the poore house hasted Amintas. 105

THE NINTH LAMENTATION.   [D1]

SInce Phillis burial now faire aurora the ninth time
Shew'd her shining face, and Phœbus lightned Olympus:
When from couch all wett with teares, confounded Amintas
Rays'd his crasd carkas, with mind stil abroad to be wan-
    dring,
Vnto the wilde-beasts dens and feareful vnhospital harbours,   5
Where was nothing els but certain death to be lookt for.
But whilst naked lims with roabs al ragged he cou'red,
Oft did he call and crie for Phillis, for bony Phillis,
With deepe sighs and grons still Phillis, Phillis he called:
And then drest, vp he gets, and gets himselfe to the desert,   10
Desert dens, mans sight, and Sunns light euer abhorring.
There by the woods wandring, and loue vnlucky bewayling,
More and more did he feede that wonted wound of a louer.
Like as a trembling hart, whose heart is pearct with an ar-
    rowe,
Runs, and yet running his death still beareth about him,   15
Runs to the thickest groues, yet sweats and bleeds as he
    runneth,
Runs, and so with toyle and greefe death hasteneth onward:
Then with teares doth he seeke Dyctamus flower by the
    desert,
Seeks, but cannot finde Dyctamus flower by the desert,
Like to the trembling hart went hartles louer Amintas.   20
And thus againe at length (his cheeks with water abounding)

101 Amintas. Amintas: A'
7 he] be C E
16 sweats and bleeds] bleeds and sweats D
17 toyle and greefe] griefe and toile C E

Talia vociferans, et sparsus pectora fletu.
   Phyllis in æternam noctem cùm clauserit orbes,
Quod nunc consilium, aut quæ iam fortuna sequatur,
Nè mea deformem subeat res tota ruinam?
25 Omnis enim census longè mihi cura recessit
[C1ᵛ] Pristina, nec possum curare à Phyllide quicquam.
Per quem nunc hyeme subdentur pabula bobus?
Aut niueo petulans addetur bucula tauro?
Per quem nunc rupis ducentur in alta capellæ
30 Candentes, matrésque lupis raptentur et agni?
Per quem nùnc vdis aries in gurgite villis
Mergetur? per quem scabies vngetur amurca,
Anteà per turbas mala quàm contagia serpant?
Per quem pungentur salientes sanguine venæ
35 In pede balantis, quandò depascitur artus
Febris, et incensas est arida flamma medullas?
Per quem molle pecus montes cogetur in altos,
Cærula cùm Thamesis pluuijs humoribus aucta,
Vel niue, non curuis ripis atque aggere sueto
40 Se cohibet, summum sed inundans æquore littus
Præcipiti, rurísque casas, et pinguia latè
Pascua deuastat, rudibus ploranda colonis?
Heu pecus, armentúmque sed eheù Phyllida raptam,
Et me Pastorem miserum, miserúmque bubulcum.
45 "Mercibus amissis qui naufragus enatat, arduo
"Illisa cymba scopulo, pontóque Notóque
"Voluitur, ignotæ fluitans per littora terræ,
"Nec videt Oebalios vsquam pia sydera fratres,
"Ille sua me sorte refert. Nam Phyllidis ex quo
50 Dura quies oculos, et somnus ferreus vrget,

    24 tota] totæ 85.
    34 venæ] vena 85.
    45 arduo] *last two letters blotted* 85.

The ninth Lamentation

From sullen silence abruptly began to be raging.
  Since Phillis lockt vp that starlight liuely for euer,
Since faire Phillis slept that long sleepe, what shal Amintas
Thinke, conceiue, contriue, or what shal Amintas imagine,   25
What shal Amintas doe, that Amintas go not a begging?
For no care is of health, no care of wealth in Amintas,
No ioy, no comfort, but Phillis abyds in Amintas.
  Who will fodder now in Winter giue to my bullocks?
Who will now any more bring my white bull to my heifer?   30
Who will goats and kidds to the ragged rocks be a dryuing?
Who will sheepe and lambs from rau'ning wooules be de-
    fending?
Who will looke to my rams, and wash their fleese in a riuer? [D1ᵛ]
Who will anoint scabb'd sheepe, least that contagius humor
Once take vent, make waie, and spoile whole flock of Amin-   35
    tas?
Who will let them bloud, when raging fire of a feuer
Runneth along by the bones, and marrow quicklie deuoureth?
Who will tender sheepe driue vp fro the fields, to the moun-
    tains,
When deepe Thames increast with raine or snow from Olym-
    pus,
Driues down wonted wals, and banks all beateth asunder,   40
Ouerflowing fields, and pastures foulie defacing?
O poore flocke, poore heard, ô life, and loue of Amintas:
Phillis life and loue is gone, ô wretched Amintas.
Eu'n as a marchant man that lost his ware by a shipwrack,
And ship left on sands with blind rocks broken a sunder,   45
Swims on a board stagg'ring with salt waues all to bedashed:
Driu'n hence thence with winds, and knows no place to be
    landing:
Wandring here and there, and sees no starre to be shining:
So twixt hope and feare, twixt life and death doth Amintas
Dailie delaie his daies, yet deathes wound beareth about him.   50
For since Phillis, alas, in a dead sleepe slipt from Amintas,

---

32 will] *omit* E   39 deepe Thames] deepe brooke D

34 contagius] outragious E   40 wonted *faults escaped*] wanted A

35 take vent] get strength D   48 starre] starres C D E

[69]

Continuò in curas animus diducitur omnes:
[C2] Et pede non stabili solus per lustra ferarum,
Per vacuas rupes, ac per pendentia saxa,
Et per inaccessos colles, colubrûmque cauernas,
55 Atque per hos lucos horrendos fronde relapsa
Fluctuo, sed nusquàm pâret mea candida Phyllis.
Me neque Sol vnquam, neque Cynthia tempore ab illo
Vel minimos gelido libantem cespite somnos
Vidit, et assiduis furari lumina curis.
60 Ieiuno rabidam stomacho depellit orexin
Virginis altus amor, qui cunctos possidet artus.
Exaturántque sitim salsi, quos sorbeo, fletus
Imbribus hybernis similes, quos humidus Auster
Nymboso exturbat luctanti flamine cælo.
65 O veneranda Pales, pastorum maxima Diua,
Cum Superûm nemo mœsti misereretur Amyntæ,
Tene etiam meriti capiunt obliuia nostri,
Cui stramentitijs totiès de fascibus ignes,
(Cum celebranda forent tua festa Palilia ruri)
70 Accendi sacros, superans incendia saltu,
Libáque magna manu Dryadis confecta dicaui,
Lacque bibens tepidum, spargens et lacte fauillam?
Tuque ingrata Venus, tuque ô damnose Cupido,
Quos totiès, mecum dùm Phyllida lætus habebam,
75 Hymnisonis toto cumulaui laudibus agro,
Admirante choro pecudum, socijsque colonis,
Cur infœlicis iam non miseremini Amyntæ?
[C2ᵛ] Nil vestras tenuisse aras, et supplice dextra
Thuricremos struxisse focos, ac dona dedisse

Inconstant, wandring, distracted, moydred Amintas
Raungeth alone by the rocks, by the woods, by the dens, by
    the deserts,
Deserts, dens, and woods, and rocks, where no bodie walketh,
No bodie dare aproch for feare of slipperie serpents,   55
And crawling Adders with balefull poison abounding.
And yet I can not find what I seeke, what I looke, what I long
    for,
Phillis I mean by the rocks, by the woods, by the dens, by
    the deserts.
   Since that time, that time of griefe and woe the beginning,
Neither sunne by the daie, nor moone by the night did Amin-   60
    tas
Euer see sleeping, though weake and wearie by watching.
And no food I desire for I feed to fast on a fancie,
Loue fils faintie stomack, and euerie part of Amintas.
And I desire no drink, for I drinke vp waterie fountains,
Fountains of salt tears, still trickling, euer abounding,   65
Like showres in winter driu'n down with winds from
    Olympus.
O most mightie Pales, which stil bar'st loue to the countrie,
And poore countrie folke, hast thou forgotten Amintas
Now, when as other Gods haue all forsaken Amintas?
Thou on whose feast daies bonefires were made by Amintas,   70
And quite leapt ouer by the bouncing dancer Amintas,   [D2]
Thou, for whose feast daies great cakes ordained Amintas,
Supping milke with cakes, and casting milke to the bonefire?
   And thou surlie Cupid, thou churlish dame Cytheræa,
With whose praise I did once, whil'st Phillis abode with   75
    Amintas,
Make these fields to resound, make beasts and men to be
    wondring,
On pitifull poore wretch is no care, no pitie taken?
What? shal I nothing get for making so manie offrings,
So manie sweet perfumes, for saying so manie praiers?

68 Amintas] B C D E; Amintas. A
69 Amintas? B C D E] Amintas, A

80 Proderit, atque caput myrti vinxisse corona?
Nullane apud Diuos veteris stat gratia facti?
Cur igitur tantis reboant altaria votis?
Immemoris quorsum colimus tot numina cæli
Credula turba nimis? virtuti (heu) præmia desunt.
85   Ast quare damno Superos, aut sydera, fixum
Cùm nequeant Superi, vel sydera vertere fatum?
Et quorsum te Phylli queror, dulcissima rerum,
Dum colles, nemus, arua, lacus indagine claudo,
Cùm neque quid fletus, neque quid sint gaudia norint?
90 At licet absenti nil proficientia verba
Profero, nequicquàm tristi tamen alloquar ore:
Et lachrymas, quanquam lachrymæ voluuntur inanes,
Prodigus effundam: Non est amor omnibus idem.
   Attamen vlteriùs desertis callibus ire
95 Non libet, ac nimiùm vitæ iam tædet acerbæ.
Ipse manu mortem inueniam, miserebitur Orcus
Sanguine conspersi: Facilis iactura sepulchri est.
Saucius errabo cum Phyllide læta per arua,
Componens manibúsque manus, atque oribus ora.
100   Sed redit angusti subter fastigia tecti.

All with a greene garland with leaues of mirtle adorned?   80
Are gods vnthankfull? can no grace come from Olympus?
Are gods vnmindfull? why then, what meane I to worship?
Worship I know not what for a god, when it is but an Idol:
For no guerdon, alas, no good thing's left for a good man.
   Poore foole, what did I meane, on gods or stars to be   85
     railing?
As though stars or gods could alter destinies order.
Poore foole, what did I meane incessant teares to be shead-
     ing?
Stil to the hils, to the woods, to the fields, to the flouds to
     be wailing?
Sith these hils, these woods, these fields, these flouds to my
     weeping,
Can lend no feeling, can aford no sense to my wailing.   90
Yet wil I call Phillis, though no bodie come by my calling,
And weepe for Phillis, though no good come by my weeping,
Thus wil I doe: manie men, manie minds: this pleaseth
     Amintas,
And yet I can not abide anie more by the woods to be raung-
     ing,
And this liuing death, this dying life to be leading: 95
Dye then Amintas, dye, let Amintas murther Amintas,
So shal that grim Sire, and foule fac'd prince of Auernus,
Some pitie take, when he sees this wound of murdred
     Amintas,
This wound wide and large: and losse of grau's but a small
     losse.
So shal Amintas walke, and Phillis walke with Amintas,   100
Through those pleasant groues and flowring fields of Auernus:
   But yet againe to his house, with doubtfull mind he re-
     turned.

80 greene garland] garland greene B C D E
84 thing's B C D E] things A   92 by my B C D E] by A
88 be] my E   100 shal *faults escaped*] shall A
89 Sith] Since D   101 Auernus *faults escaped*] Amintas A
91 wil *faults escaped*] will A   102 doubtfull] dolefull E

[C₃]   *QVERELA DECIMA.*

Iamque dies decima emicuit, socíjque senilis
Et gelidi pertæsa thori Palantias atra
Nubila discussit, venienti præuia Soli,
Et Cephali cupidis se submissura lacertis.
5   Æolus, Auroræ qui demulceret amores,
Laxabat Zephyrum, et qui sub rorantia molli
Gramina siccaret flatu, nè frigidus humor
Noctis amatorum furtiuos læderet ignes,
Paruus et Æolides nè non daret oscula Diuæ.
10 Omnia ridebant, syluæ, agri, flumina, cælum,
Ruráque mulcebat cantu campestris alauda,
Atque hilares duxêre noua sub luce choræas
Pulchricomæ Charites, lata et saltâre per arua
Lasciui Satyri, canna ludente palustri.
15 Solus at exosus tam lætæ gaudia lucis,
Matutæque iocos, gemitus fletúsque ciebat
Incassùm Pastor,* et rupit pectore questum:
Desertóque statìm tecto, lucósque subintrans,
Ereptam tali clamabat Phyllida voce.
20   Heu, Phylli quid agis? quid non reminiscere nostri,
Noctes atque dies pro te qui pectore crudum
Vulnus alo? quarè solam iuuat ire per vmbras
Lætantes? niuei pecoris num pristina cura

17 *asterisk indicates a short syllable where meter requires a long one*

THE TENTH LAMENTATION. [D2ᵛ]

SInce that fatall day and houre vnlucky the tenth time
Faire Aurora betimes by the dayes break rose from her hus-
band,
Husband old and cold, and droue darke clouds from Olympus,
Making way to the sunne, taking her way to the yonker,
Braue yonker Cephalus, whome faire Aurora desired. 5
Æolus, of purpose, auroraes fancie to further,
Sent forth sweete Zephyrus with tender breath to be blowing,
And moist deaw by the fields with whistling blast to be
drying,
Least nights colde moisture might stay their louly proceed-
ings,
Stay braue Æolides, stay braue Aurora fro kissing. 10
Euery thing did smile, woods, fields, ayre, watery fountains,
Euery lapwing sang, and made sweete myrth to the morning,
And cheereful Charites with goldlocks gaily bedecked,
Daunced along by the fields in due and gratius order:
And th'vnruly satyrs by the sound of a paltery pyper, 15
Leapt and skipt by the woods, in most lasciuius order.
Only Amintas loath'd these sports, and these prety pastimes,
Only Amintas mourn'd, and olde griefs only remembred,
Leauing house and home, and deserts only frequenting,
Scratching face with nails, and Phillis freshly bewailing. 20
O what means Phillis, can Phillis cast of Amintas?
O consider, alas, consider careful Amintas,
And forget not, alas, forget not faithful Amintas,
Who for Phillis sake, for loue and fancie to Phillis,
Bears this fire in his heart, and still this fire is a feeding. 25
What means Phillis alone in those faire fields to be walking,
In those Elysian faire fields, and leaue me behinde her?
What's there no more care of flock in Phillis abyding? [D3]

3 darke] backe C E clouds] cloads A
12 Euery lapwing sang] Euery Lark did sing D   to] of C'
21 Amintas? B C D E] Amintas. A
26 Phillis alone] Phillis, alas, D
28 flock] a flock E

Nulla manet? tibi nulla mei quoque cura relicta est?
25 O nimis ingratam, si sit tua culpa, puellam;
[C3ᵛ] Et crudele nimìs fatum, si cogeris illo.
Aspice quàm vigili curæ deuotus Amyntas
Interea, et nudo quàm pastoralia desint
Omnia. Non vltrà pecudes in pascua pello,
30 Phœbus ab Eoïs quandò caput exerit undis:
Sed nec vimineis septis includo capellas,
Phœbus in Herculeis quandò caput occulit vndis.
Porrò septifora ad celebrandas canna choræas,
Carmina iamque mihi desunt festiua; pedúmque
35 Ampliùs haud gesto curuum; non sessilis obba
Ad latus affixa est corio pellisuè caprina,
Quæ femoris primam decoraret pendula partem,
Deseruítque vagæ catulus vestigia plantæ,
Latratu tenerum qui custodiret ouile.
40 Aspice quàm pereant te nunc absente capellæ,
Queis thyma nemo manu blanda, dulcésque liquores
Præbet, et exustas feruenti syderis æstu
Sub gelidas umbras ducit, stabulisué reponit.
Aspice quàm pereant te nunc absente bidentes,
45 Nec me fungente officio pastoris: agresti
Præda lupo fiunt erepti matribus agni;
Et scabies mala tentat oues; illotáque sordent
Vellera, nec sordes quisquam sub flumine mersat.
Sed vereor cælo stolidus nè murmura iactem,
50 Dum placidas inter nymphas in rure beato
Elysia vallis maius tu pascis ouile
[C4] Immemor (heu) nostri gregis, et languentis amici.
Ergò sola mei mors est medicina doloris?
Nec tamen ante diem fas est concedere morti?
55 O duras hominum sortes, heu tristia fata.
Attamen insano iuuet efferuescere motu,
Et miserum peiora sequi meliora probantem.
Scilicet infirmos dum spiritus hos reget artus,
Hæc mea perpetuus cruciabit viscera planctus,

53 medicina] medecina 85.

What? no care of loue, no care of louer Amintas?
O vnthankfull wench, if this thing come by thy causing,   30
And accursed fate, if desteny cause thee to leaue mee.
  See what a strange effect these cares haue wrought in
    Amyntas
Needeles cares haue driu'n all needefull cares from Amintas.
No care, no comfort in driuing goats to the mountains,
When rising Phœbus displayes his beames in a morning.   35
No care, no comfort in bringing sheepe to the sheepe coats,
When sitting Phœbus withdrawes his face in an euning.
Rimes are quite set a side, and seu'nhol'd pipe is abandond,
Rimes that I playd on pipe: pipe vsed at euery dauncing.
Leather bottel's lost, and tarrebox broken a sunder,   40
Shoone, and mittens gone, and sheephooke cast in a corner,
And little olde Lightfoote hath lost his maister Amintas,
Whose watchful barking made wolues afraide to be byting.
See, how Phillis death doth make my goates to be dying.
No body giues them time and other flowers to be gnapping,   45
No body giues them drinke and water fresh to be sipping,
No body brings them backe to the folde, or shade to refresh
  them.
  See, how Phillis death doth make my sheepe to be dying,
Whilst th'vnlucky sheepheard neglects his sheepe to be
  feeding,
Lambs in woful wise by the wolues are daily deuoured,   50
Ews in loathsome sort with scabbs are fowly molested,
And their wooll with dust and durt is filthily fowled.
O but, alas, poore foole, whilst thou thus rayl'st on Olympus,
Phillis faire, perchaunce in pleasaunt fields of Auernus,
Keepeth better goats, and better sheepe is a feeding,   55
Leauing this poore flock, and their poore maister Amintas.
And must onely my death cause endles plagues to be ended?
And shal I neuer die, till time that desteny pointed?
O what a life is this, with life and death to be striuing?
And yet I loue this life, this strife, and euery moment   60
Reason yeelds to my rage, and rage giues place to my reason.
And whilst breath shal abide in burning breast of Amintas,
Perpetual sobbing shal make these sides to be smarting,

56 flock] flcok A

60 Hæc mea perpetuas resonabunt ora querelas,
   Hæc mea perpetuo turgebunt lumina rore.
   Lux quotiès aderit terris, et ab æquore Titan
   Hesperio, gemitu ventoso nubila cogam:
   Nox quotiès operit terras humentibus vmbris,
65 Innumeris vastos augebo fletibus amnes.
   Ecquis erit, nostro qui se conferre furori
   Possit amor, cui nulla dies, aut hora quieta
   Illuxit, postquam mea candida Phyllis abiuit?
      O crudelis Amor, qui maxima causa fuisti
70 Exitij, læthíque mei, qui prima fuisti
   Causa, quòd his oculis aspecta virgine plures
   Conciperem flammas animo, quàm Sicilis ipsa
   Eructare solet disruptis Ætna caminis.
   Quis te crediderit pastori velle nocere
75 Innocuo? sed et arma geris, mentémque tyranni.
   Tuque O sæua nimìs Rhamnusia rebus opimis
   Inuida, deceptrix hominum, Dea lubrica semper,
[C4ᵛ] Quid tibi cum nostris erat ignibus? oscula nostra
   Quid numen læsere tuum? quid ludicra verba
80 Per multas horas protracta sub arbore? vel quid
   Mutuus amplexus, vel binæ copula mentis?
   Ruricolæ fuimus, mundi pauperrima turba.
   Sunt orbi magis apta tuo diademata regum
   Aurea, quæ multi sunt ponderis: alta rotare
85 Conuenit, et turres pedibus calcare superbis.

   68 candida] candtda 85

Perpetual playning shal make this mouth to be sounding,
Perpetuall weeping shal make these eyes to be swelling.   [D3ᵛ]
As soone as Titan with face all fyrie returneth,
With violent clamors great clouds wil I cast on a cluster:
As soone as darke night doth spread her mantle among vs,
With teares stil trickling Ile make springs euer abounding.
What lou's like to my rage? what fancy's like to my folly?   70
That not a day, not an houre, not a moment scapeth Amyn-
    tas,
But stil Amintas mourns, since Phillis graue was a making.
  That lewd Lord of loue drew my destruction onward,
That boy bred my bane, my death vntimely procured,
When by the sight of a lasse, by the flaming eyes of a virgin   75
Fire did pearce by my flesh, to my soule, to my bones, to
    my marrow,
And there burns and boils like scalding sulphur of Ætna.
Who would thinke thou loue couldst beare such hate to a
    louer?
Or wouldst worke such harme to a countrieman that is
    harmeles?
But bloody boy thou art, thou bear'st bloody mind, bloody   80
    weapons.
And thou most spiteful Nemesis, whose hasty reuenging
Hands are euer at hand: whose minde is mutable alwayes,
At miseries laughing, at mens felicitie grudging,
Why durst thou deale with? what didst thou meane to be
    medling
With louing Phillis, with Phillis louer Amyntas?   85
If that Phillis I kist, or Phillis kissed Amintas,
If that Phillis I clipt, or Phillis clipped Amintas,
If that I spent many houres in talking vnder a myrtle,
Wast any great offence, any great disgrace to a Goddesse?
We were countrie folke, two seelly'st soules of a thousand,   90
Those golden diadems, that state of a king, or a kingdome,
Those vaunting titles, that pompe of a duke, or a dukedome,
Those flaunting buildings, that pride of an Earle or an earl-
    dome,
More fitt for Nemesis: Phillis more fitt for Amintas.

  88 If that] If I E   92–93 *omit* D

Quis te crediderit pastoribus esse nocentem
Innocuis? fera sed stat pro ratione voluntas.
   Tuque ô Parca ferox Furijs immanior ipsis,
Vndè animum subijt sceleris tam dira cupido,
90 Vt matura viro moreretur et innuba Phyllis?
Ergonè sperabas sua tollere gaudia ruri?
Ergoné credebas miseros consumere curis
Agricolas? neque te virtus, neque lucida forma
Inflexit? nostri neque sanctum fœdus amoris?
95 Quis te crediderit caprimulgæ posse nocere
Innocuæ? sed sæua malis, et sanguine gaudes.
Cur autem mihi non mutilas quoque licia mortem
Optanti toties? Certum est iam velle perire,
Vt lætos habitare queam cum Phyllide lucos.
100   Attamen in tectum cœpit sub nocte reuerti.

[C5]   *QVERELA VLTIMA, ET A-*
       MYNTÆ EXITVS.

Funereis nymphæ post ignibus ossa cremata,
Vndecimo colles cùm lumine sparsit oborto
Fulgida Tithoni coniux: insomnis Amyntas
E tecti tegulis vt primùm albescere lucem
5 Vidit, inops animi strato surrexit, et ægro
Ædibus excedens passu, vestigia flexit
Lubrica per virides campos ad triste sepulchrum

Who would thinke thou couldest on beggers thus be triumph-   95
    ing?
Why should seelly shepheards be molested thus by a God-
    desse,
Nay Godlesse Nemesis? for thou doest no body goodnes,
And where's no goodnes, who thinks there can be a Goddesse?
And thou most hellish Lachesis, more fierce then a fury,
What reason foundst thou such mischiefe for to be working,   100
That by the griping pains, by the colde hoate fitts of an ague,
Phillis fitt for a man, should die thus afore she be fitted?   [D4]
O why shouldst thou take all comfort quite fro the countrey,
And make countrie men thus comfortles to be mourning?
Could not that sweet face, nor that most seemely behauiour,   105
Nor that league of loue stil lasting leade thee to mercie?
Who would think that thou wouldst haue thus delt with a
    milkmaid?
But thy delight is death, and bloud thou only desirest,
Therefore bring me to death, take liuing bloud from Amintas,
For my delyte is death; death onely desireth Amintas,   110
And to procure quicke death, it's fully resolu'd by Amintas,
That faire Phillis againe may loue her louer Amintas.
    And yet about euning, with staggring stepps he returned.

THE LAST LAMENTATION,   [D4ᵛ]
AND THE DEATH OF AMYNTAS.

ANd now since Phillis dead corps was laid in a coffin,
Came th'eleuenth daie, when weake, yet wakeful Amintas
Spi'd through tyles of his house, faire Phœbus beames to be
    shining:
Which when he saw, then in hast himselfe he began to be
    stirring,
And with trembling knees, with mind extreemlie molested,   5
Passed along to the fields, where graue of Phillis apeared:

107 haue thus] thus haue C E; D *omits line*
113 returned] retyred D

2 Came th'eleuenth daie] Twelfth day came at last D   yet] and E

Virginis: vt mutum ad cinerem, mânésque silentes
Funderet extrema ferales voce querelas.
10　Quà postquàm teneros flores, graménque nouatum
Conspexit, charúmque suæ sibi nomen amicæ
Insculptum, et nullo moriturum tempore carmen:
Quamuìs, heu, paulùm lachrymis, et mente moratus,
Mox tamen incubuit tumulo, genubúsque reflexis
15　Sic effatus erat, cygni morientis imago.
　　Hæc lux, hæc tandem vitæ lux vltima, longis
Questubus imponet finem, mihi meque meámque
Restituet, multos vincet mors vna dolores.
O dilecte pater, genitrix ô charior, ô vos
20　Pastores mihi grata cohors, fidíque sodales,
Ædite venturo nullos in funere planctus,
Quandoquidem iubet ipsa Venus succumbere morti,
Et me tardantem placidis expectat in aruis
[C5ᵛ]　Alma anima optatæ, non ipso flexilis Orco.
25　At mihi si quicquam debetis, cæca serate
Lumina frigenti, et cum Phyllide cespite eodem
Obruite, ambobus summum hoc concedite nobis.
Tuque gregem nostrum in campos charissime Damon,
Ne mecum pereant, Tuque ô Amarylli, capellas
30　Phyllidis in virides tecum deducito montes.
Est mihi nam certùm crudelem abrumpere vitam,
Et lætari alia vita sub morte reperta.
　　O tandem syluæ, vites, iuga, flumina, valles,
Et vitrei fontes, et cætera cuncta valete:
35　Posthàc non questus vobis miserantibus ægros
Exercebit amans, aut suspirabit Amyntas
Ampliùs. Ergonè me memet mactare necesse est

The last Lamentation

Meaning there to the graue, to the ghost, to the scattered
    ashes,
His last lamenting in wofull wise to be making.
But when he saw fresh flowres, and new grasse speedilie
    start vp,
And Phillis sweet name ingrau'n by the hand of Amintas,   10
Then did he stay and weepe with an inward horror amased:
And at length his knees on graue there faintilie bowing,
With dolorus gronings, his fatall howre he bewailed.
  This day, this same day, most blessed day of a thousand,
Shall be the first of ioy, and last of anoie to Amintas,   15
This shal bring me my selfe to my selfe, and bring me to
    Phillis.
Let neither father, nor mother mourne for Amintas,
Let neither kinsman, nor neighbour weepe for Amintas,
For Venus, onelie Venus, doth laie this death on Amintas,
And Phillis sweet soule in faire fields staies for Amintas.   20
If you needs will shew some signe of loue to Amintas,
Then when life is gone, close vp these eies of Amintas,
And with Phillis corps lay this dead corps of Amintas,
This shall Phillis please, and Phillis louer Amintas,
And thou, good Damon, driue forth those sheepe of Amintas,   25
Least that Amintas sheepe die with their maister Amintas.
And thou faire Amarillis, when thou gang'st to the moun-
    tains,
Driue on Phillis goats, faire Phillis goats to the mountains:
For now tis certaine, Ile leaue this life for a better,
And seeke for mending in a most vnnatural ending.   30
Hils and dales farewel, you pleasant walks of Amintas,
Wells and fludds farewell, sometime the delyte of Amintas,   [E1]
Now shal I neuer more my sorrowes vtter among you,
Now shal I neuer more with clamors vainly molest you.
Must then Amintas thus but a stripling murder Amintas?   35

25 Damon] Thyrsis D

27 faire Amarillis] good Daphne D

29 now tis certaine] now it's certaine B C E; now, at length, D

32 Wells and fludds] Fluds and wells B C D E

In D lines 31–34 follow line 64 of "The Eleventh Day." See appendix.

[83]

Immaturum annis? heu, quanta potentia regni
Est Venus alma tui? Postquam mea Phyllis abiuit,
40 Non oculis vnquàm somnos, aut pectore noctem
Accepi: nec enìm languorum tædia possum
Plura pati, ingeminant curæ, rursúsque resurgens
Sæuit amor: sed nunc sanabo vulnere vulnus,
Hæc erit et miseræ vitæ, et lux vltima luctus.
45   Ergò vbi concepit furias, et versat in imo
Corde dolos, dirúmque nefas, et fluctuat æstu,
Decreuítque mori: Nocuit differre paratis,
Inquit, et extracto, quem secum fortè gerebat,
Cultello, primùm cæli conuexa tuetur,
[C6] Tum gemit, et pallens hæc verba nouissima fundit:
    Parcite iam, Superi, supremáque parcite Mânes
Tentanti: flammas ferro, ferróque furorem
Feruidus auertam, licèt improba fata recusent,
Teque sequar Phylli. Media inter talia cultro
55 (Heu) diro infixus cecidit, terrámque manúsque
Sanguine fœdauit: Tellus miserata cadentem
Molliter excepit, sed et ipsa gemente sub illo
Increpuit, luctum tristi testata fragore.
    Cælicus intereà, quamuis maiora Senatus
60 Tractaturus erat, tamen hæc spectacula cernens
Indoluit, subitòque animam migrare iubebat
Sub noctem, lætóque frui cum virgine campo:
Corpus Amaranthi formámque et prendere nomen,
Ac placidos noti ruris florere per agros.
65   Talia dum statuunt illi, frigentia lætho
Lumina labuntur, sensímque in sanguine sensus
Euolat, et tremulos paulatìm deserit artus.

The last Lamentation

O what an imperious princesse is Queene Cytheræa?
For still watching loue would neuer let me be resting,
Nor neuer sleeping, since Phillis went from Amintas.
And no longer I can susteine these infinite horrors,
And pangs incessant, which now are freshly renewed,   40
And much augmented: therefore am I fully resolued
Of lingring lou's wound to be speedily cur'd by a deaths
    wound.
Thus when he had contriu'd in his heart this desperate out-
    rage,
And meant fully to die, with an hellish fury bewitched;
What do I stay, quoth he, now? tis losse of time to be lin-   45
    gring.
Then with a fatall knife in a murdring hand; to the heauens
Vp did he looke for a while; and groan'd with a deadly re-
    sounding,
With these words his life and Lamentation ending.
   Gods, and ghosts, forgiue, forget this fault of Amintas,
Pardon I craue of both: this knife shall bring me to Phillis,   50
And end these miseries, though desteny flatly deny it.
Eu'n as he spake these words downe fell deepe wounded
    Amintas,
Fowling hands and ground with streames of bloud that
    abounded.
And good natur'd ground, pytying this fall of Amintas
In most louing wise very gent'ly receiued Amintas   55
And when he fell, by the fall, in mournefull sort she re-
    sounded.
Iupiter in meane time, and th'other gods of Olympus,
When they saw his case (though great things were then in
    handling,)
Yet lamented much, and then decreed, that Amintas
Soule, should goe to the fields where blessed Phillis abideth,   60
And bloody corps should take both name and forme of a faire
    flowre
Called Amaranthus; for Amintas friendly remembrance.
Whylst these things by the gods wer thus decreed in Olympus,
Senses were all weake, and almost gone from Amintas,
Eyes were quite sightles, death pangs and horror aproched: 65

[85]

Iamque pedes subita, caput inclinatus Amyntas,
Suspiransque altùm, queritur radice teneri,
70 Pesque vbi sit quærit, nusquam tamen inuenit illum.
Vtráque nam tibia, et corpus languore liquescens
Vertitur in viridem culmum: gelidúsque medulla
Pristina fit succus, siccámque humectat aristam.
Brachiáque ad cælum supplex dum tendit, acutas
75 Induit in spicas: restabant ora, comæque,
[C6ᵛ] Quid facitis Superi, mussat, (nam debile vocis
Murmur erat) quarè non est data copia mortis?
O Superi, mussabat adhuc, mussantiáque ora,
Atque comæ pulchri floris traxêre figuram,
80 Hæserúntque noua tristes in arundine voces.
Est rubor in folijs, scires è sanguine nata.
    Iamque pharêtratus solio surrexit ab alto
Diuus Amor, seròque sui miseratus Amyntæ,
Talia voce tulit Superûm auscultante corona.
85   Populus Alcidæ cordi est, et myrtea matri
Sylua meæ, et Cereri segetes, et laurea Phœbo,
Et grauidæ Baccho vites, et oliua Mineruæ:
Noster Amaranthus iam flos erit, omnibus illis
Pulchrior; vndantémque sua virtute cruorem
90 Sistet, quantumuis è sanguine duxerit ortum;

Then with his head half vp, most heauily groned Amintas,
And as he gron'd, then hee felt his feete to the ground to be
    rooted,
And seeking for a foote, could finde no foote to be sought for.
For both leggs and trunck to a stalk were speedily chaunged,
And that his olde marrow to a colde iuyce quickly resolued, [E1ᵛ]
And by the same cold iuyce this stalk stil liuely apeared.
Which strang chang when he felt, then he lifted his arms to
    the heauens,
And when he lifted his arms, then his arms were made to be
    branches.
And now, face and heare of Amintas lastly remayned,
O what meane, you gods, to prolong this life of Amintas?   75
ô what meane you gods, with an hollow sound he repeated,
Vntil his hollowe sounde with a stalk was speedily stopped,
And faireface and heare bare forme and shape of a faire
    flowre,
Flowre with faire red leaus, faire red bloud gaue the begin-
    ning.
Then with bow and shaft and painted quiuer about him   80
Vprose Lord of loue, from Princelike seate in Olympus,
And when 'twas too late laments this losse of a louer,
Speaking thus to the gods of this newe flowre of Amintas.
Myrtle's due to Venus, greene Laurell's due to Apollo,
Corne to the Lady Ceres, rype grapes to the yong mery   85
    Bacchus,
Popplar t'Alcides, and Oliues vnto Minerua,
Gentle Amaranthus thou fairest flowre of a thousand
Shalt be my floure henceforth, and though thou cam'st from
    a bleeding,
Yet bloud shalt thou staunch: this gift will I giue thee for
    euer:

67 felt] left B C E	84 due] deare D
78 shape of] shape to E	85 rype grapes] and vines D
80 shaft] shafts D	86 *omit* D
82 'twas] t'was A laments C D E] lament's A B	87 Gentle Amaranthus thou fairest] But thou fayre Amaranthus, gentlest D

Querela vndecima

Hoc feret à nobis: illósque per omnia campos
Sæcula purpurei folij circundabit ostro,
In quibus ereptos dudum plorauit amores:
Virginibus capita, et pueris, ludóque paratas
95 Ornabit Charites; et flos dicetur Amoris.
    Intereà absentem longo iam tempore Amyntam
Per saltus vacuos, obscuros perque recessus
Syluarum, per et antra feris horrenda, cauásque
Rupes, et gelidas valles, montésque, lacúsque
100 Ruricolæ frustrà quærunt, et vana queruntur.

FINIS.

And by the pleasant fields where gentle minded Amintas   90
Lately bewaild his loue, there thy leaues louely for euer
Boyes, and gyrles, and nymphs shal take a delyte to be
     plucking,
Take a delight of them their garlands gaye to be making.
And now in meane time whylst these things were thus a
     working,
Good louing neighbours for a long time missed Amintas,   95
And by the caues of beasts, by the dungeons darke, by the
     deserts,
And by the hills, by the dales, by the wells and watery foun-
     tains,
Sought for Amintas long, but neuer mett with Amintas.

FINIS.

90 fields] parke D
91 leaues B C D E] leau's A
97 by the dales] and dales D

[*89*]

In inuidum quendam, sub Oli
nomine, quem taxat Mar-
tialis.

EPIGRAMMA.

Antigonen Sophoclis malè vertimus? Ole quid ad te,
  Quid faciat versu nostra Thalia suo?
Peccaui patrijs in rithmis? Ole quid ad te?
  Non tua, quæ scripsit, sed mea pluma fuit.
5 Vulnus amatori sanauimus? Ole quid ad te?
  Est illo solus carmine læsus Amor.
Non dignè psalmos transcripsimus? Ole quid ad te?
  Non tua propterea, sed mea fama perit.
Phyllida tam ploro iuueniliùs? Ole quid ad te?
10 Non tua, quam ploro, sed mea Phyllis erat.
Noster hiat versus, vel claudicat? Ole quid ad te?
  Forsan at exemplis linea nulla caret.
Seria nulla typis committimus? Ole quid ad te?
  Cùm libeat, dabimus seria multa typis.
15 Liuescit tibi cor; hoc ad te pertinet, Ole.
  Illa rudis, quæ sunt candida, carpis: et hoc.
[C7ᵛ] Quæ tu scribis, olent: hoc ad te pertinet, Ole.
  Mendax in tota plebe vocaris: et hoc.
Tu sciolum dicunt: hoc ad te pertinet, Ole.
20 Tu medio digito sæpè notaris: et hoc.
Quæ tu dissimulas ad te spectantia, cuncta
  Si numerem, numero cedet arena maris.

FINIS.

TRANSLATION OF EPIGRAM

Against the sort of envious person Martial reproaches
under the name of Olus.

Did I translate Sophocles' Antigone badly? Olus, what's that
    to you;
  What should my light Muse do with his verse?
Have I sinned against traditional meters? Olus, what's that
    to you?
  It was not your pen but mine that wrote it.
Did I heal a lover's wound? Olus what's that to you?   5
  Love alone is injured by that poem.
Didn't I transcribe the Psalms well? Olus, what's that to you?
  For that reason my reputation, not yours, is suffering.
Do I now in a very youthful way lament Phyllis? Olus, what's
    that to you?
  The Phyllis I lament was not yours, but mine.   10
Are my numbers defective? Olus, what's that to you?
  Still there is no line without a precedent.
Do I never publish serious things? Olus, what's that to you?
  When I feel like it, I'll print many serious things.
You have an envious heart; this has something to do with   15
    you, Olus.
  You clumsily slander innocent things: and this too.
What you write stinks: this has something to do with you,
    Olus.
  Everybody calls you a liar: and this too.
They call you a coxcomb: this has something to do with
    you, Olus.
  People often gesture at you with their middle finger: and   20
    this too.
If I counted the people you pretend admire you,
  The number would exceed the sands of the sea.

Appendix

Major Authorial Changes in "The Second Part" of
The Countesse of Pembrokes Yuychurch (1591)

From the Epistle, Signature A2:

IF Amyntas *found fauour in your gracious eyes, let* Phillis *bee accepted for* Amyntas *sake. I haue somewhat altered S.* Tassoes *Italian, and M.* Watsons *Latine* Amyntas, *to make them both one English. But* Tassoes *is Comicall, therefore this verse vnvsual: yet it is also Pastoral, and in effect nothing els but a continuation of* æglogues, *therefore no verse fitter than this. For such as generally mislike this reformed kinde of verse, as I spake before, so I say stil. . . .*

Lines added at the beginning of the "First Lamentation"—here called "The First Day"—in order to tie it to the pastoral play preceding. Signature G1:

NOw bonylasse *Phillis* was newly betroathd to *Amyntas*
By rich *Montanus* consent; whoe yet, for a long tyme
Wedding day differd, til his owne byrth day was aproach-
    ing:
That twooe solempne feasts ioynd fryendly togeather in one
    day
Might with more meryment, and more concurse be adorned.   5
   Soe men on earth purpose, but Gods dispose in *Olympus:*
For, when as each thing was by the Father duly prepared,
And byrthwedding day now nere and nearer aproached,
Wedding by brydes death was most vntymely preuented,
And fathers byrth-day, deaths-day to the daughter apoynted; 10
Deaths-day lamented many dayes by the woeful *Amyntas,*
Deaths-day which hastned deaths-day to the mourneful
    Amyntas:
Whose mournyng all night all day, did weary the
    Mountaynes. . . .

[93]

Appendix

In a footnote following "The Third Day" Fraunce supplies this commentary on lines 8–10, Signature H1:

> Eccho could not now to the last woord yeeld any Eccho
> All opprest with loue, for her ould loue stil she remembred,
> And she remembred stil that sweete Narcissus her ould loue, etc.

Some litle men fynde great fault, that this word, *stil*, being twice vsed, is but an idle repetition to make vp the verse. Where, if they could see, that in the first place it is an Aduerb, and an Adiectiue in the second, they might as well bee stil, and not speake any thing, as stil talk, and yet say noething.

Between the "tenth" day and "The Last Lamentation"—here "The Twelfth Day"—Fraunce adds "The Eleuenth Day." These verses give a good idea of Fraunce's style when he is imitating rather than translating:

[K3]   *THE ELEVENTH DAY.*

NOw th' eleuenth day from death of *Phillis* aproached,
Which to the former rage that long possessed *Amyntas*,
Dogged new conceipts with more resolution added.
   And shal I stay, quoth he, now? shal I wayte for greater
     aboundance
5 Of sowle-tormenting horrors? shal I stil be a dying,
And yet liuing stil? Did I thrust my brest on a poynted
Dart, when *Phillis* liu'd, though *Phillis* fled from *Amyntas*?
Yea, did an vntrue tale, did a heare-say woork in *Amyntas*
Soe, that he threw himself fro the hill topp desperat, head-
     long,
10 Hearing *Phillis* death by *Fuluia* falsly reported?
And shal *Amyntas* now, when he knows, when he sees, when
     he looks on,
Lookes on *Phillis* alas, and see's her fayntyly gasping,
Lookes, and sees her alas, her last, last breath to be yeelding,
Lookes, and sees those eyes with fathers hands to be cloased,
15 (Eyes by *Amyntas* his hands more worthyly for to be cloased)
Lookes, and sees, (dead sight) her sacred face to be cou'red,

And corps embalmed; shal hee now, now feare to be dying?
  Daphne stayd darts-wound, and causd it, not to be deaths-
    wound,
Desteny made downefall for that tyme not to be mortall;
But neyther *Daphne*, nor cursed Desteny hencefoorth   20
Shall withdraw this knife from bleeding brest of *Amyntas*.
  Yf *Daphne* could not, nor cursed Desteny would not
Keepe *Phillis* from death; why should they keepe me fro
    Phillis?
  Once it was my chaunce my naked louely *Diana*
For to behould by the well; but alas my louely *Diana*   25
Her poore *Actaeons* true loue vnkyndely requyted,
And freed *Phillis* did fly from freer *Amyntas*.
  Afterwards, forsooth, our wedding day was apoynted;
Apples tutcht my chyn, to my lipps streames louely   [K3ᵛ]
    aproached;
But when *Tantalus* hoapte his fruyte and streames to be   30
    tutching,
Apples fled fro my chyn, fro my lipps streames louely retyred,
Brydall by buryall was most vntymely preuented.
Now, if woorse doe remayne, let come, let come to *Amyntas*
Ere that *Amyntas* dy, for he meanes noemore to be trifling,
But this self-sacrifice to the sweetest Saint to be offring.   35
  Goe poore Sheepe and Kydds, sometyme the delite of
    Amyntas,
Seeke now somewhere els both boughes and grasse to refresh
    you
Make your way by the fyelds, and neuer staye for *Amyntas*,
Lodg your selus at night, and neuer looke for *Amyntas:*
Some pytyfull goodman wil take compassion on you,   40
And feede you wandring, and bring you home by the eu'nyng:
Now shal I neuer more your hornes with flowrs be adornyng,
Now shal I neuer more your selus to the fyelds be a dryuyng,
Now shal I neuer more see you creepe vp to the Mountayns,
Now shal I neuer more sitt downe and sing in a valley.   45
Thinck it noe strange thing if Woolus dooe chaunce to
    deuoure you,
Sith that Woolues are lyke to deuoure your master *Amyntas*,

[95]

Vnles some good man this carkas chaunce to be cou'ring.
  Goe poore louing dogg, ould Light-foote, seeke thee a
    master,
50 Get thee a new master, since thyne ould master *Amyntas*
Gets hym an other dogg, fowle *Cerberus* horrible helhounde.
Now shal I neuer more geue Light-foote bones to be gnawing,
Now shal I neuer more cause Light-foote, glooues to be
    fetching:
Yf, for thy feeding from a whelp, thou meane to be thankfull,
55 Then keepe rau'nyng Woolus from wounded corps of
    Amyntas.
  Pype, fitt for meryment, vnfitt for mourner *Amyntas*,
Hang on this myrtle, til good luck send the a master,
More blessed master, than tentymes cursed *Amyntas*.
  Roses fayre and red, which *Phillis* lou'd to be wearing,
60 Keepe stil fayre and red, keepe fresh and louely for euer,
My red blood shal stil geue new supply to the rednes.
  Yuychurch farewell; farewel fayre *Pembrokianaes*
Parck and loued lawndes; and, if fayre *Pembrokiana*
Scorne not my farewel, farewell fayre *Pembrokiana*.
65   Hills and dales farewell, you pleasant walks of *Amyntas*,
Floods and wells farewell, sweete looking glasse of *Amyntas*.
Now shal I neuer more my sorrows vtter among you,
Now shal I neuer more with clamors vaynly molest you.
[K4]   Handkercher farewell, sweete work of my bony *Phillis*,
70 Handkercher many tymes made moyst with teares of
    Amyntas,
Now shal thy Gelyflowrs; which wanted nought but a rednes,
Proue perfect Gelyflowres; my blood shal geue them a rednes
Soe shal *Phillis* woork in part be the woork of *Amyntas*.
  Hart of gold, farewell, which *Phillis* gaue to *Amyntas*,
75 Signe of a louing hart, which greeues my heart to be leauing:
And would neuer leaue, vnles that I meant in a moment,
This my liuing hart, and hart of gold to be leauing.
  Wedding ring, farewell, shee's gone, whose yuory finger
Should haue been thy grace: ful well did I cause to be grauen
80 In thy golden round, those words as true as a Gospell,
Loue is a bitter-sweete, fit woords for bitter *Amyntas*.
  Farewell knife at last, whose poynt engrau'd in a thousand

Appendix

Barcks of trees that name, sweete name of my bony *Phillis*,
And hard by that name, this name of Louer *Amyntas*:
Soe that in euery ash, these names stood, *Phillis Amyntas*   8ʟ
And each Beech-tree barck, bare these names, *Phillis
     Amyntas*:
Pastors dayly did ask, what folk are, *Phillis Amyntas?*
Nymphs did dayly demaund, who wrote this, *Phillis
     Amyntas?*
But now, loued knife, thy paine is somwhat abridged,
Now write *Phillis* alone, and noemore, *Phillis Amyntas*:   9c
Now write *Phillis* alone; but let not an ash, or a beech-tree
Beare soe blessed a name, which only belongs to *Amyntas*:
My brest shalbe the barck, write *Phillis* name in *Amyntas*:
And since sharpned poynt shal finde soe tender a subiect,
Strike, engraue, cut, launse, spare not to be mightily wound-   95
     ing:
Let faire *Phillis* name to the eyes of louely beholders
With blood-red letters in *Amyntas* his hart be apearing.
     Yet this murdring stroake to an other time he referred.

*Lines added at the end of "The Last Lamentation"—here "The
Twelfth Day":*

Downe in a dale at last, where trees of state, by the pleasant [Lɪᵛ]
Yuychurches parck, make all to be sole, to be sylent,   100
Downe in a desert dale, *Amaryllis* found *Amaranthus*,
(Nymph, that, *Amyntas* lou'd, yet was not lou'd of *Amyntas*)
Founde *Amaranthus* fayre, seeking for fayrer *Amyntas;*
And with fayre newe flowre fayre *Pembrokiana* presented.   105
     Who, by a strayte edict, commaunded yearely for euer
Yuychurches Nymphs and Pastors all to be present,
All, on that same day, in that same place to be present,
All, *Amaranthus* flowre in garlands then to be wearing,
And all, by all meanes *Amaranthus* flowre to be praysing,   [L2]
And all, by all meanes his *Amyntas* death to be mournyng.   111
     Yea, for a iust monyment of tender-mynded *Amyntas*,
With newfound tytles, new day, new dale she adorned,
Cal'd that, *Amyntas* Day, for loue of louer *Amyntas*,
Cal'd this, *Amyntas* Dale, for a name and fame to *Amyntas*.